Laying the Ghost

A play

Simon Williams

Samuel French — London
New York - Toronto - Hollywood

LAYING THE GHOST

First presented by The Mill at Sonning Dinner Theatre, with the following cast:

Freda Deacon	Heather Chasen
Margot Buchanan	Caroline Blakiston
Mrs Kidd	Carolyn Lyster
Sadie	Sarah Grochala
Lady Buchanan	Lucy Fleming
Leo Buchanan	Francis Matthews
Superman	Willie Liam
Orderley	Sam Grainger

Directed by **Kit Thacker**
Set design by **Jacqueline Hutson**
Costumes by **Jane Kidd**
Lighting by **Matthew Biss**

The play takes place in the sitting area of Yew Tree House, a retirement home on the South Coast

ACT I   10.30 am on a Spring morning

ACT II   Three minutes later

CHARACTERS

Freda Deacon, an elderly actress
Mrs Kidd, the home administrator
Margot Buchanan, an actress
Sadie Croft, a young actress
Sir Leo Buchanan, an actor
Lady Judy Buchanan, Leo's wife
Superman, an unwelcome visitor

The play is set in a retirement home on the South Coast

Time—the present (2001 - some dates may need to be changed in the dialogue to accommodate later productions)

Other plays by Simon Williams published by
Samuel French:

Kiss of Death
Nobody's Perfect

ACT I

The sitting area of a retirement home, Yew Tree House, on the South Coast

There is an assortment of chairs and tables, a zimmer frame, and the walls are decorated with one or two bits of theatrical memorabilia. There is a conservatory leading off the french window L, also a corridor from the main body of the home, from which we feel slightly detached, at the end of a wing, say

Freda Deacon is one of the oldest residents and has an unkempt, rather eccentric appearance; she is wearing a headset, listening to the shipping forecast which she periodically echoes. She has a highback chair and table UR *(maybe in the conservatory), where she keeps her "bits", at another more communal table there is her jigsaw puzzle of* The Full Monty. *She is highly active, always busy and flitting about*

Margot Buchanan's usual chair is beside a substantial table where she keeps her stuff: a small telescope or opera glasses, a magnifier, a pile of papers, a cordless telephone/ansaphone, wine gums, make-up, a notepad, etc.

Spring sunshine and daffodils in vases—the distant drone of a floor polisher... That is the scene

Freda Channel Light Vessel... Visibility poor. One thousand and ten, rising slowly. White, Sole, Lundy... (*Against invisible interruption*) Quiet. Ssssh. Not now... Fastnet, Portland... (*She gives in and takes off her headset. She addresses the invisible interlocutor*) No point in going to the chiropodist, Vincent, there is nothing they can do for you.

During the following, Mrs Kidd enters, overhearing

You're supposed to have shuffled off your mortal coil and that includes your wretched verruca.
Mrs Kidd Good morning, Miss Deacon. Got a visitor, have you?
Freda No, no. It was nothing. Morning.
Mrs Kidd It's that time of the month I'm afraid. (*She gives her a bill*) Your bar bill.
Freda Oh, no. I'm skint. How much?

Mrs Kidd £108.59p. Have you seen Mrs B? I don't want her seeing the *Daily Mail*.

Freda Good idea. We all hid ours at breakfast, so we should be OK. She's in the library doing a crossword with what's-his-name with the leg.

Mrs Kidd We don't want her seeing Sir Leo like that, do we? (*She looks at a copy of the newspaper*) It's not a very flattering photo, is it?

Freda (*looking at her copy*) It always used to be two fingers for a V sign… Is this new one-fingered thing European, do you suppose?

Mrs Kidd Poor man. Imagine being hounded like that by the paparazzi.

Freda Nobody knows where the hell he is. I'm told he may have gone to ground in his native Wales.

Mrs Kidd By one of your cronies on the other side?

Freda No, by that girl on *The Big Breakfast*, they seemed to think there was a floosie involved. A love nest even.

Mrs Kidd (*smitten*) He's obviously a very naughty man in his way. Libidinous and unruly, I should say.

Freda The man is a rat. Anyway, we don't want Margot getting upset today of all days.

Mrs Kidd Exactly, we'll keep it hush hush. I've got some more birthday cards for her. Bless her. We don't want her big day ruined.

Freda No, it'd put her in fearful bait. Remember when they did his *This Is Your Life* she threw her butterscotch yoghurt at the telly. There's no point in being pally with an ex I say. I hated all mine.

Mrs Kidd rattles a small money box on the table

Mrs Kidd Her swear box is nearly full as it is. Perhaps I'm not charging enough.

Freda Fifty p for the F word is a bit steep, I reckon, but ten p a pop for the B is a bargain.

Mrs Kidd Well, I know what you actors are like. (*She studies Freda's jigsaw*) What have we got here, then?

Freda *The Full Monty*. The trouble with men is they are all so exactly alike in the nude.

Mrs Kidd Up to a point, Miss Deacon. We all have to be grateful for small mercies.

Mrs Kidd exits

Freda (*referring to the jigsaw*) Don't be filthy, Vincent. Nobody is asking you for your opinion. Waft off.

The phone rings on Margot's table. Freda hesitates and then answers

(*Into the phone*) Hallo... Yes, this is Margot's telephone. ... She's busy.
... Who am I? I'm nobody, maybe even a wrong number. Who are you?
... You can't be—she doesn't have a husband. Well, her ex-husband is that
perfectly frightful, so-called movie star, Leo Buchanan—whoops. That's
you, is it? ... I'm sorry. ... Why are you speaking in that funny voice? ...
On a train? Here? ... No, she doesn't wish to see you. ... I just know she
doesn't. She hates you. We both do. I'm her best friend. ... Yes, she does.
Because you're horrid and your films are terrible. (*She hangs up indignantly.
To Vincent*) Huh. An evil old witch.

During the following, Mrs Kidd enters, hearing her

An evil old witch, I ask you...
Mrs Kidd Found a friend, then, have you, Miss Deacon?
Freda No. As a matter of fact, that was him, Sir Leo, on the telephone.
Wanted to come and pay Margot a visit.
Mrs Kidd Here?
Freda She hates him anyway.
Mrs Kidd I don't think she does.
Freda What about the painting, then?
Mrs Kidd The Augustus John?
Freda Yes, when she heard he'd sold it, she didn't speak for three days, not
even to her bookmaker.

*Margot enters. She is elegantly dressed in designer jeans and a silk shirt.
She goes to her table and puts down a pile of cards*

Happy birthday, darling.
Margot I could kill you, Freda. You should never have told everyone. It's
going to be a perfectly ghastly bloody day. Cakes and speeches and God
knows what.
Mrs Kidd Champagne for all the residents before lunch.
Margot Ronnie Machin says he's booked a kissogram for me.
Freda A kissogram?
Margot Superman is going to come and give me a big wet kiss.
Mrs Kidd It's all right, Mrs B. I made him cancel it.
Margot Good. The last thing I need is a big wet kiss from some total stranger
in red tights. He's an unspeakable little nerd. I'm allowed nerd, aren't I?
Mrs Kidd I think so. I thought Mr Machin was your friend.
Margot He's not.
Mrs Kidd You play bridge together.
Margot That's not the same thing at all, Mrs Kidd. Just as a matter of interest,
how stupid does everyone around here think I am?
Freda Compared with whom, darling? Why do you ask?

Margot Well, all over the building every single copy of the *Daily Mail* seems to have gone into auto-destruct. Apparently copies have been lost, damaged, defaced, burnt and apparently even vomited on because of the porridge. What do you make of that?

Freda It tasted all right to me. We didn't want you to see it.

Margot I'm pretty well blind anyway, so I ask myself what news can there be in the *Daily Mail* that you all need to protect me from? Hm? Have they doubled the betting levy? Did Brighton and Hove Albion lose their play-off with a penalty shoot-out? *Or* is it perhaps good old Leo?

Freda Yes, of course it's Leo.

Margot Is he dead?

Freda No.

Margot Don't tell me he's got an Oscar?

Freda (*showing her the* Mail) No, there.

Margo studies it with her magnifying glass

Mrs Kidd We thought it best you didn't see it, that's all.

Margot Oh dear, he does look cross. Cross and old. Is he drunk? Is that *his* finger in the foreground.

Freda Yes. It's a kind of one-legged V sign.

Mrs Kidd It's the Italian version, I believe.

Margot What's he been up to, then? Read it to me.

Freda Must I?

Margot Yes. Go on.

Freda (*reading from the* Mail) "Sir Leo Buchanan responded angrily to rumours about his personal life, at the premiere of his latest film *The Sheriff of the Universe,* in Glasgow last night. When he was asked if he had any comment to make, the Welsh actor responded by swinging a punch at a journalist from a Sunday tabloid newspaper".

Margo shakes her head in silence. Mrs Kidd offers her the swear box

Margot *Che stronzo. Ein Dumkopf. Quel salaupard.*

Mrs Kidd I call that cheating.

Margot It's odd, isn't it, that he's grown old without actually growing up. So it's *cherchez la femme* again, is it?

Freda Hunt the bimbo was what they said.

Mrs Kidd (*opening the paper*) And there's his wife, on page five... Smiling bravely as she gets into her Mercedes convertible. "Lady Buchanan stands by her man". She does look a bit peaky, mind.

Margot I bet she does—the cow. I'd like to kick her teeth in.

Mrs Kidd He was on the Michael Parkinson show the other day... He was ever so funny.

Margot gives a withering look

Not funny at all. He is attractive, though, isn't he?

Another look from Margot, who is opening a card

Boring—ugly. Silly me.
Margot (*having opened a card*) What's this one say, Mrs Kidd? It's a cartoon, is it?
Mrs Kidd Yes. Actually it's rather rude.
Freda Rude. Good. What's it say?
Mrs Kidd It's not appropriate.
Margot It's a man, is it, talking to a woman. He seems to be begging. Read it out.
Mrs Kidd He's saying... I can't...

The other two urge her on

He's saying: "I promise you, Rosemary, fellatio is good for cellulite".
Freda That is funny, isn't it, Margot?
Mrs Kidd "For a v. v. v. faberoony lady on her big day. Loadsa luv, Dunc".
Margot The theatrical agent with a heart of pure lead. It's funny when you get to my age people stop saying many happy returns—I suppose they think it's tempting fate.
Mrs Kidd No gloom today, Mrs B. I'm not allowing it.
Margot I wasn't being gloomy. Today is my No-Lose birthday.
Mrs Kidd How do you mean?
Margot When they did my heart job four years ago I said to myself if they cock it up and I pop my clogs I'll have been sold a bit short, but after seventy, after today, I'm in credit—it's all jam... Hell's bells.

The phone rings on Margot's table. She answers it

This is Margot Buchanan's answering machine—I'm either dead or on the loo, please leave a message and I'll probably forget to call you back. Speak after the beep. (*She puts the receiver down and presses a button on the machine so we hear the reply*)
Male Voice (*on the phone*) Hallo ... er ... Hallo. Is that you, Margot Buchanan? Hallo... Hallooo.
Margot (*aside to Mrs Kidd*) I'm not falling for that.
Male Voice (*on the phone*) It's Graham Latimer here, I'm with a certain Sunday newspaper...
Margot (*aside*) That usually means the *News Of The World*.
Freda It's him—the man Leo punched. Graham Latimer.

Male Voice (*on the phone*) I wanted to talk to you about Sir Leo. As his first
wife, I wonder if you'd care to talk to us about his current débâcle. What
advice would you give him? What comment would you make…? Hallo?

Margot snatches up the receiver

Margot (*into the phone*) *As* his first wife it's "no comment". … What? OK,
then: "No comment, scumbag". (*She hangs up*)
Freda Ghastly little turd.
Margot The gutter press?
Freda I meant your husband.
Mrs Kidd I hope it's not the little man who was skulking about by the front
gates.

Mrs Kidd's pager goes off. She picks up Margot's phone

Excuse me. (*Into the phone*) Hallo, Doreen? … Oh, right. Thank you. I'll
come and get her. (*She hangs up*) That's your visitor arrived, Mrs B.
Margot Visitor? What visitor? I'm going back to bed.
Mrs Kidd Sadie Croft… You are expecting her? You're not expecting her?
She's an actress … going to play Juliet.
Margot (*rummaging among bits of paper*) Bugger. Bugger. Bugger.
Mrs Kidd Now Mrs B, you're only allowed six a day. Isn't that rather
wasteful?
Margot (*counting in 10p coins*) Bugger. Bugger. Bugger. There. I might
even have to borrow a few from tomorrow. (*Holding up a scrap*) Is that it?
I meant to put her off.
Mrs Kidd (*reading*) "Two pounds, E. W. Lady Cynara, two forty-five,
Newbury."
Margot I thought I answered her letter. Why why why do we let ourselves
in for this purgatorial kind of thing—I hate young people…
Mrs Kidd You do not.
Margot Mark my words, she'll be in black from head to toe with a ring in
her nose and clumping great shoes.
Freda Grungy. That's the word you're after.
Margot Grungy? Can't you tell her I've gone gaga. (*She passes another
scrap of paper to Mrs Kidd*) How about this?
Mrs Kidd Vaseline, wine gums, the *Spectator*. I'll go and fetch her.
Margot (*holding up a lipstick*) I'd better tart myself up a bit. What colour
is this?
Mrs Kidd Cherry red. I'm off. I'll take this for you.
Margot Hmm?
Mrs Kidd Your list: Vaseline, wine gums, the *Spectator*.

Mrs Kidd Your list: Vaseline, wine gums, the *Spectator*.

Margot Bless you. I'm a complete hedonist, aren't I?

Freda (*to Vincent*) Will you shut up. (*To the others*) Sorry—it's poor old Vincent, he's got a verruca.

Mrs Kidd (*joking*) Well, it won't kill him, will it? You put your headphones on and take no notice. (*To Margot*) I'll get you a pile of 10p coins too. I have a feeling it's going to be a busy day.

Mrs Kidd exits

Margot scrutinises some lipsticks

Margot You really must be more careful about your "visitations". You know she doesn't approve. What colour is this?

Freda You mean she'll have me banged up in the funny farm. A tarty pink.

Margot (*handing it to Freda to apply*) That'll do.

Freda Where do you want it?

Margot Where do you think? Ghosts aren't everyone's cup of tea, you know.

Freda Well, they're not mine either, I don't enjoy being harangued morning noon and night by a lot of dead old actors.

"Vincent" gooses her and she reacts

Get off. Behave. Vincent says "Happy Birthday" too, by the way.

Margot Yeah, well, if in doubt, you stick to the shipping forecast and do your jigsaw.

Freda I'm a bit stuck actually—it must be thirty years since I saw a man in the nude. I'd forgotten how untidy all their bits look. (*She applies the lipstick*) Does my breath smell?

Margot Yes, of course.

Freda So does yours.

Margot What is cellulite, anyway, I thought it was a kind of telephone.

Freda It's fat, darling. How the hell am I supposed to find £108.59p for my beastly bar bill. (*She applies the finishing touches*) There we are. Lovely.

The phone rings and Margot picks it up

Margot (*into the phone*) Can't be bothered. Leave a message. Bye. (*She puts the receiver down*)

Leo's Voice (*on the phone*) Hallo... It's me. Leo. Long time no ... no see... If you're there, Margot, pick up the phone, please... Please...

Margot's hand reaches out and Freda restrains her

Freda No. No. No.

Leo's Voice (*on the phone*) I just spoke to some mad old crone who said you
   wouldn't speak to me... Margot, please, for old time's...

Margo cuts him off

Freda Well done.

Margot He rang earlier, did he?

Freda Yes.

Margot And you weren't going to tell me?

Freda What's the point? I didn't want you getting upset. How about some
   rouge?

Margot Blusher. What the hell can he be up to?

Freda God knows.

Margot Who cares anyway?

Freda You do.

Margot You're quite right, of course, he is a ghastly little turd, always was,
   but he does...

Freda Have a way with him?

Margot Something like that. He's like an old allergy... I keep thinking that
   I might be over it, that I might have become immune, but I only have to see
   a photograph of him or hear his voice and all the old symptoms are there.
   The irritation, the nausea, the foreboding...

Freda The quivering knee, the sweaty palm. So if ... say ... for instance, he
   turned up here ... you'd tell him to bugger off?

Margot If I had the 10p I'd try. He ought to carry a health warning: "This
   bastard can seriously damage your peace of mind".

Freda Absolutely. (*She starts to sing a line from "I'm Gonna Wash That
   Man" from* South Pacific)

Freda joins in with her

   *Sadie Croft enters. She is young and pretty. She is dressed not in black and
   not in clumpy shoes. No ring in her nose. She does wear an engagement
   ring and carries a bag containing a mobile phone*

They see her and stop in mid-flow

Sadie I was told to come on through.

Margot Ah. You must be...

Sadie Sadie Croft.

Margot Of course. Good. Yes. This is Freda Deacon.

Sadie (*recognizing her*) Not *the* Freda Deacon?

Freda No. Probably another one.

Margot How do you do?

Freda It's her birthday.

Sadie Today? I had no idea. Congratulations. I'm surprised you didn't cancel our meeting.

Margot Good Lord, no. I've been looking forward to meeting you, haven't I, Freda? (*With the telescope or opera glasses*) Let me look at you.

Freda (*retreating into her headset*) Excuse me. I've got to see a man about a verruca.

Sadie She was in *Yon Bonny Banks*, wasn't she, on the telly? I thought she was dead.

Freda (*without turning*) Not quite.

Sadie I'm so sorry.

Margot They treat her for schizophrenia because nobody likes believing in ghosts. It's about as helpful as giving an alcoholic an Alka Seltzer.

Sadie How much can you see exactly?

Margot Not enough to read or sew, but enough to dial a friend or find Radio 4.

Sadie How miserable.

Margot Yeah. Well, when the good Lord shuts down one of your five senses, he sharpens up the other four. You're from the West Country?

Sadie Wow. I see what you mean. I was born in Barnstaple. Are you sure you want to do this? (*i.e. have a chat*) I mean you don't have to.

Margot I'm not sure I'll be any use to you, it's over forty years since I played Juliet.

Sadie With Leo Buchanan as your Romeo.

Margot That was him.

Sadie Your husband.

Margot Briefly.

Sadie In his biography, P. J. Monckton says your Juliet to his Romeo was the most electric evening of his theatre-going life. He said the emotional heat between the two of you on the first night was palpable.

Margot Yes, well, he was a *very* discerning critic. Is that why you came? To see if you can find out how it was done? When do you start?

Sadie Next month. In Leeds.

Margot The old Grand?

Sadie The new Playhouse.

Margot Of course. And the production?

Sadie Elizabethan, set in Verona.

Margot Good. Directed by...?

Sadie Sheila Almond.

Margot Very à la mode. And your Romeo?

Sadie Barnie Alsop.

Margot Don't know him. Dark?

Sadie Yes.

Margot Good. Romeo should be dark. Is he sexy?

Sadie Ish.

Margot Ish? He should be dripping in it. How long is the tour?

Sadie Four months.

Margot So you'll have an affair with him.

Sadie Is it inevitable?

Margot No, but it'll help pass the time.

Sadie I don't think so.

Margot You're attached, then?

Sadie Sort of.

Margot Sort of? You mean he's married.

Sadie It's mostly a platonic thing.

Margot Platonic? In my day that just meant sex after lunch. Was it he who gave you the Ysatis?

Sadie (*sniffing her own wrist*) Yes.

Margot It used to be my favourite too.

Sadie Not any more?

Margot I'm not in the business of alluring nowadays.

Sadie So why were you putting on make-up when I arrived?

Margot I didn't want to scare you.

Sadie You wouldn't have, your face is so...

Margot Please don't say "well preserved".

Sadie It's hardly changed at all. I was at Sotheby's last month when they auctioned the Augustus John... The one of you in the rose garden.

Margot makes no attempt to answer

I just loved it ... you looked so...

Margot Foolhardy.

Sadie No... Sort of invincible.

Margot dismisses this

You weren't tempted to buy it?

Silence

Didn't you like it?

Margot I can't talk about that. It was a long time ago... So.
  (*As Juliet*) "O, I have bought the mansion of love,
        But not possessed it..."
Don't you love that line. Go on. From there.

Sadie   (*as Juliet*) "…and though I am sold,
Not yet enjoyed; so tedious is this day
As in the night before some festival
To an impatient child that hath new robes
And may not wear them…"

Margot Very nice.

Sadie Shall I go on?

Margot No. Please don't. I know how it ends. The thing is to keep it simple, isn't it? Juliet is simple, straightforward. She's naturally happy, don't you think? That's what makes her tragic… Always have more breath than you need… Hm? New breath, new thought. That's why it's called inspiration.

Sadie That's very good.

Margot It's just technique. It gives you spontaneity.

Sadie Of course. What else?

Margot Don't look at the floor—look up, to the great blue yonder, that's where thoughts come from, even the sad ones. It's also better for those poor suckers in the cheap seats. (*She looks through the telescope or opera glasses*) Don't scowl either. Juliet doesn't scowl and neither should you. Juliet has her eyebrows up. (*She demonstrates*) Up for innocence and hope. Down for puzzlement and irritability.

Sadie What about the passion?

Margot Passion. Huh. Let's start with love. Tell me, Miss Mostly Platonic, what do you think love is?

Sadie You tell me.

Margot Love is about recognition, the recognition of what someone can do for your self-esteem. The key to life is self-esteem.

Sadie Is that what made for the palpable heat between you and Sir Leo? Or was that just technique too?

Margot No, that was something else.

Sadie It says in the book his leaving you broke your heart.

Margot Yes and no.

Sadie How do you mean?

Margot He didn't leave me, I threw him out. And my heart had a congenital weakness anyway.

Sadie It can't have been easy though.

Margot Compared to giving up smoking, it was a cinch.

Sadie The show must go on and all that.

Margot (*shaking her head*) No, it shouldn't. The theatre doesn't heal old wounds, you know, it seeks them out and rubs salt in them. Remember that.

Sadie So you're not in touch with him, then?

Margot Nope. (*Flaring up*) Look, of all the topics of conversation on God's earth, Leo Buchanan is the one I would most like not to discuss. OK? He's a… He's a… Yes?

Freda (*with her hand up*) A ghastly little turd.

Sadie Oh, I'm so sorry—I didn't realize.

Margot What? What didn't you realize?

Sadie Nothing.

Margot I'm sorry. Did I frighten you?

Sadie No.

Margot Then I'm losing my touch. After Juliet, you should have a go at Viola, then Rosalind; before you know it, you'll be playing Cleopatra.

Sadie You never played Cleopatra, did you?

Margot No. That's one of my regrets.

Sadie What others do you have?

Margot Ha. Wouldn't you like to know. I'd like to have been in an action film with Clint Eastwood. I could have worn a leather jacket and dug a revolver into someone's ribs and said "shut the fuck up". Is that a split infinitive, do you suppose?

Sadie Who cares?

Margot Yes. Shall we do a bit more? You're going to be quite good.

Sadie You sound surprised. Aren't I quite what you were expecting?

Margot No. I thought you might be grungy.

Sadie Huh! And I thought you might be gaga.

"Grungy" and "gaga" laugh

Mrs Kidd enters

Mrs Kidd I'm sorry to interrupt. But Lady Buchanan is here to see you… Mrs Buchanan.

Margot I beg your pardon?

Mrs Kidd Lady Buchanan has come to pay you a visit.

Margot Lady Buchanan? Here? Is this a joke?

Mrs Kidd No.

Margot I thought you said you'd cancelled the kissogram.

Mrs Kidd Shall I bring her in?

Margot Oh, bollocks.

Mrs Kidd That'll cost you 20p, Mrs B.

Margot Twenty?

Mrs Kidd They come in pairs, I believe. 10p each.

Judy, Lady Buchanan enters. She is a very attractive middle-aged woman

Margot scrutinises her with the telescope or opera glasses

Judy I thought if I rang ahead, you'd probably say you were busy, so I thought I'd come by and say hallo or something.

Margot (*cold as ice*) Or something.

Judy And Happy Birthday, of course.

Freda (*oblivious—at her jigsaw*) No, Vincent, what I need is a nice bit of hairy buttock...

Mrs Kidd (*diverting her*) Freda... This is Lady Buchanan, Freda Deacon. And this is...

Sadie Sadie Croft. How do you do?

Judy How do you do?

Sadie I'd better go...

Freda (*to Judy*) Welcome to Yew Tree House. Have they put you in Nora Ramone's old room?

Judy Good Lord, I'm not here to stay. I'm not a resident, thank you.

Freda Never mind. (*To the invisible Vincent*) Nora was a very naughty girl, wasn't she, Vincent?

Judy is confused at the lack of Vincent

Mrs Kidd Would you like a coffee, Lady Buchanan?

Judy Thank you.

Mrs Kidd Mrs Buchanan?

Margot I'd like a brandy.

Judy Make it two, please.

Freda So you two are sisters, are you?

Judy ⎫
      ⎬ (*together*) No.
Margot ⎭

Margot Lady Buchanan is married to Leo, Freda.

Freda Oh, I see. You're wives-in-law. (*To Judy*) You looking for him, are you? He's got his knickers in a bit of twist, hasn't he? He's not here. We haven't got him, have we, Margot?

Mrs Kidd Headphones, Miss Deacon. I'll get the drinks. Two brandies. (*She makes to exit. To Sadie*) Shall I make it three?

Sadie shakes her head but Freda indicates "three" by holding up three fingers

Mrs Kidd exits

Judy Did I interrupt something?

Sadie We were just doing some work on *Romeo and Juliet* actually.

Judy Lovely. I remember seeing my husb... Oh, Christ.

Margot Lady Buchanan was going to say she remembers seeing Sir Leo and me in the 1958 production at *The Globe*. When she was five.

Judy I hadn't imagined putting my foot in it quite so badly or quite so soon.

Margot Feel free.

Sadie I'm going to play Juliet, she was giving me some advice.

Sadie I'm going to play Juliet, she was giving me some advice.
Judy Well, good luck. I hope it goes well.
Sadie Thanks. I think I'll just go and make a telephone call.

Sadie exits

Judy and Margot eye each other in silence

Freda (*to her companion*) No, Vincent, this is not going to be fun.
Margot Headphones, darling, nice and loud.

Freda complies

The recently dead use her as a sort of *Yellow Pages.* She can't hear us, she's perfectly——
Freda (*without turning round*) Harmless. Sorry, everybody.
Margot Quite. Why don't you sit down?
Judy Thank you. (*She sits*) Look, you mustn't think I don't know you don't like me.
Margot My oh my, all those negatives. Well, I don't.
Judy What?
Margot (*feeling her pulse*) Think you don't know I don't like you.
Judy What are you doing?
Margot Checking my pulse. I have a bad heart. It doesn't like surprises. Or Marmite or cheddar cheese.
Judy I just came to wish you Happy Birthday.
Margot Did you? Now I really am curious.
Judy In what way?
Margot Call me cynical, but isn't this a search party—haven't you rather mislaid your husband?
Judy When Leo goes into hiding, the best way of finding him is not to go looking, did you never learn that?
Margot Then I can't see why you should drive all the way down here from Chalfont St Giles just to wish me Happy Birthday.
Judy I bought you a card. It may relieve your curiosity.
Margot Surely you could have sent it, Lady Buchanan.
Judy (*putting the card on Margot's table*) There's no point in asking you to call me Judy.
Margot (*binning the card*) Absolutely none.
Judy Would you like me to go?
Margot You can cartwheel stark naked down the corridor for all I care.
Judy Oh, that is very droll. You see, that's what's so good about show business, you don't just say "go away"—you dress it up with a little quip, a jocular remark.

Margot Don't let my sunny nature mislead you.

Judy I think it's a good sign—you trying to be witty.

Mrs Kidd enters with the three brandies and delivers them

Mrs Kidd Here we are then, ladies, three brandies. You all getting on all right? Will you be staying to lunch, Lady Buchanan?

Margot No...

Judy Thank you.

Freda (*to poor Vincent*) I don't give a toss about your verruca.

Margot Freda!

Freda Yes?

Margot Volume.

Freda Up?

Margot Down. Radio up. You down.

Freda Right-ho.

Mrs Kidd I'll leave you to it, then.

Mrs Kidd exits, a little worried

Judy It's St Peter, by the way.

Margot What?

Judy It's Chalfont St Peter where we live, not Chalfont St Giles. You were right of course, your birthday was just a pretext. It's been quite some time since we first met though—face to face.

Margot Twenty-eight years.

Judy Exactly, it's etched in my memory. And I just thought perhaps we ought to see if there isn't some cut-off point on your disdain for me—your dislike—your hatred, call it what you will.

We hardly notice Margot writing something on a notepad

Margot Hatred is fine with me.

Judy Come on, Margot. Let it go, huh? What do you say? Free yourself of it, this cancerous loathing.

Margot You say our first meeting is etched in your memory.

Judy Yes. In every detail.

Margot This is when I walked in and caught you in bed with Leo.

Judy Yes.

Margot May the 12th, 1973.

Judy You said you hoped I'd rot in stinking putrefaction.

Margot (*feeling her pulse*) Did I? Well, that just goes to prove that not all wishes come true.

Judy I do get athlete's foot from time to time, if that's any consolation. (*Referring to Margot's pulse*) How is it?

Margot It's fine. Do we really need to take this trip down memory lane? You may find this hard to believe, but my dislike, my cancerous loathing of you has nothing to do with Leo. I dislike you in your own right—I can't explain it. I know you have many wonderful qualities, I've read about them in *Hello* magazine, but I just don't like you. It's the same with spaghetti bolognese, I know all the ingredients are absolutely fine and dandy and lots of people love it, but I simply hate spaghetti bolognese. You think it's bad for me to go on hating you, I tell you I've grown accustomed to it the way an old house gets used to its ivy. So, if it's OK with you, I'll just carry on.

Judy You say it has nothing to do with Leo?

Margot Not a bit. You're welcome to him.

Judy You always thought he'd come back to you.

Margot I wouldn't have had him.

Judy Oh, no?

Margot He's gone off anyway.

Judy What's that supposed to mean?

Margot Those new teeth for a start. He looks like Bugs Bunny. It's none of my business, but I think he's missed his potential.

Judy So does his knighthood count for nothing, then?

Margot Not a jot—it's like giving an old car an MOT these days.

Judy He's one of our great actors.

Margot No. He damn well is not a great actor. *The Sheriff of the Universe* is not great acting, it's just tacky.

Freda I thought we weren't supposed to be talking about *him*.

Margot Shut the fuck up, Freda.

Judy I don't believe I heard that.

Margot (*inserting five 10p coins in the swear box*) It was a birthday treat to myself.

Judy You are truly cantankerous, aren't you?

Margot I'm doing my best.

Judy And you can honestly say it has nothing to do with the selling of the Augustus John?

Margot looks away

Now we're coming to it.

Margot puts a number of coins in the pot

Margot (*with restraint*) Go away, Lady Buchanan. Leave me alone.

Judy It was Leo's painting. His to sell.

Margot It was of *me*. It was my face. My father's rose garden.

Judy There is something I'd like to say about that...

Margot Please don't.

Judy So the spaghetti bolognese has no right of reply?

Margot Why can't you come clean, Lady Buchanan. Own up, you have not come here to wish me Happy Birthday, you have not come here to bury the hatchet, you've come here to see if I've any idea where your husband is.

Freda If you ask me, he should go back to the proper old English V sign.

Margot Back to the jigsaw, Freda.

Freda Sorry. (*She obeys*)

Margot I wouldn't tell you anyway.

Judy (*picking up the jotting pad*) May I see what you wrote? (*She does*) Bugger off isn't normally hyphenated, is it?

The phone rings on Margot's table. She picks it up

Margot (*into the phone*) Hallo, this is Margot Buchanan's answering machine... (*She looks at Judy*) Oh, no, it's not. (*Into the phone*) Hallo. ... What? Oh my God... (*She covers the mouthpiece*) Freda. (*Loudly*) Freda.

Freda It's not supper, is it?

Margot Perhaps you could take Lady Buchanan to the bar.

Freda Got you. I've got my nipples all in a muddle anyway. (*She takes Judy's arm*) Come with me. Have you ever had a Ghostly Premonition? It's a new cocktail I've invented—mostly gin.

Freda and Judy exit

Margot (*into the phone*) Hallo. ... Yes, I am. Quite alone... Well, I do not—repeat not—want to have a little chat with you.

Leo Buchanan appears very quietly in the conservatory—he is extremely elegant, all in black. As he first appears he is actually wearing a false beard and tinted glasses. He puts down a big bag in the conservatory. He speaks into a mobile

Leo (*into his mobile*) I just wanted to wish you Happy Birthday.

Margot (*into the phone*) Is that all? I'm very busy.

Leo (*into his mobile*) You don't look very busy.

Margot (*looking round, astonished*) What the hell...

Leo (*on his mobile*) It's me. (*He takes off his beard*) Leo.

They talk to each other by telephone across the room

Margot What the hell are you doing here?

Leo I came to wish you Happy Birthday.

Margot Why the beard?

Leo I'm on the run.

Margot From the *News of The World*?

Leo Chap called Graham Latimer.

Margot Aren't you rather old to go hitting people?

Leo He was quite small. I think he might have followed me. I'm in a bit of a mess.

Margot Hard cheese, please go away.

Leo I want to talk to you.

Margot I do not wish to speak to you. Clear off. Goodbye. (*She hangs up*)

Leo follows suit

Leo Margot… (*Cut off*) That wasn't very friendly… I must say it's good to see you, old thing. Are you cross? Of course you're cross. I'd be cross.

Margot disregards him

I'd be really cross if I turned up here without warning me, after all these years in the middle of my birthday. Seventy, eh? You look terrific. Lovely.

Margot peers at him through her telescope or opera glasses

"But soft, what light through yonder window breaks." … You'd get a better view if you had that thing round the other way…

Margot slams the telescope or opera glasses shut and continues to look away

It's not bad here, is it? Light and cosy… (*He picks up her betting slip*) The two-thirty at Newbury—Lady Cynara fell at the second to last. (*He screws it up*) Bad luck.

Margot will not look at him. Leo moves to the jigsaw and hits the redial button on his mobile

Good Lord, how can you face this sort of thing so soon after breakfast. They're big boys, aren't they? Mind you, if it turns you on, fair enough.

Margot's phone rings and she answers it

Margot (*into the phone*) Hallo? Yes?

Leo (*into his mobile*) Margot, please, I haven't got time for you to go through a full-scale sulk. Please, can't we just fast-forward to the monosyllabics.

Margot hangs up indignantly. Leo disconnects. His ploy has failed

I give up, it's your turn to speak now. You must be bursting with witty little remarks. Your famous scathing badinage. Come on, Margot, for goodness sake say *something*.

Margot What?

Leo "Sit down. Take your coat off. Do you want a drink?"

Margot (*without grace*) "Sit down. Take your coat off. Do you want a drink?"

Leo Thank you. Actually, I've got a flask here. Do you fancy a drop? "Oh, all right then."

Margot Oh, all right then.

Leo (*pouring two drinks*) Actually, I was frightened you might throw something. A vase or a fit. "Why would I do that?"

Margot Why would I do that?

Leo Because of the Augustus John.

Margot turns and stares at him

It's been sold. Auctioned. (*He waits*) Did you know?

Margot says nothing

You're upset? Or, you don't give a damn.

Margot (*quietly*) Go away.

Leo Yeah. OK. Well, we won't talk about that. (*He picks up the jotting pad*) You knew I was coming, then? Rather quaint to hyphenate it. (*He drinks*)

Margot It was written to your wife.

Leo (*appalled*) To Judy? Judy here? Judy came here?

Margot Yes. She's in the bar.

Leo Here. Oh my God. The mind boggles. You wrote bugger off to Judy and she obeyed?

Margot She's having a drink with Freda Deacon in the bar.

Leo Good Lord, Freda Deacon, I thought she was dead. She's looking for me, of course?

Margot (*nodding*) Of course, she *said* she'd come to wish me Happy Birthday, to make peace.

Leo Peace? Judy doesn't make peace. What kind of peace?

Margot You know peace—as in "Peace in our time". As in *War and Peace*. Peace.

Leo My God, that must have been a shock for you. I'm so sorry. I mean you haven't seen her in the flesh since…

Margot 1973. No. She looks better, mind you, with her clothes on.

Leo Cheap. Were you rude to her?

Margot Good Lord, no.

Leo I'm speechless.

Margot Not you, surely. You who can do dialogue for two. (*She would never admit that she's having a wonderful time*)

Leo The thought of it has brought me out in a cold sweat. What did you talk about?

Margot You know, this and that—what you were like in bed.

Leo Oh my God. Anything else?

Margot I told her I didn't like your new teeth.

Leo My teeth?

Margot She seemed to think they came with your knighthood.

Leo And how did you leave it?

Margot Well, they're your teeth. Look, why the hell don't you just take her home and leave me alone.

Leo I bet you can't remember anyway.

Margot What?

Leo What I was like in bed.

Margot It's thankfully wiped from my memory. Mr Woodpecker.

Leo (*chuckling*) Mr Woodpecker.

Margot Go home, Leo. I'm an old woman with glaucoma and a dodgy heart and the last thing I need is you turning up here uninvited after all these years, disguised as Rolf Harris.

Leo You're loving every minute of it.

Margot Not one jot.

Leo Secretly deep down, though, you're actually quite pleased I came.

Margot No. Secretly deep down I'm actually in a blinding rage that you came.

Leo How about superficially, then?

Margot Why, I ask you, after a thirty year absence, should I have to put up with the shambolic pile of crap that passes for your life being dumped in my lap, the mystery, the intrigue, the paparazzi and that maddening ghastly woman? You ask me if I remember what you were like in bed—the answer is I remember what you were like out of it. You are a nightmare, Leo. You are an appalling man—vain, cowardly, egotistical, duplicit, callow, and ... what's that other one they use for Cabinet Ministers?

Leo Sleazy.

Margot Exactly. Jolly sleazy.

Leo Have you finished?

Margot No. Yes. No. Go back to Glasgow or Chalfont St Bloody Giles or your blasted bimbo and leave me in peace.

Leo Bravo. I'd forgotten how brilliantly ludicrous you get when you're cross, my darling. All pompous and high-blown and sexy as hell.

Margot You are an abomination. And don't call me darling.

Leo Why not?

Margot It's either theatrical, or it's insincere. Either way I don't like it.

Leo (*re-filling her glass*) It's neither.

Margot Bugger off.

Leo You know what's happened to you—you've got old.

Margot That's what time does to people, for God's sake. Some of us manage it with a little dignity. Now please, go away.

Leo It was stupid of me to come to you for sympathy, I suppose. What's wrong with my teeth anyway?

Margot Oh my God. You've stopped smiling, that's all. Those awful films.

Leo Don't be ridiculous. Of course I smile. I never stop. The Sheriff of the Universe smiles all the time. Look. (*He salutes*) "Defend the galaxy with pride, kiddo".

Margot (*with the telescope or opera glasses*) That's more of a wince. With your old crooked teeth you used to have a marvellous smile, especially at the curtain call. Roguish and humble at the same time. Irresistible.

Leo I still do. Of course I smile. There's nothing wrong with my teeth.

Margot Of course not, they just need running in a bit. Do it for me.

Leo What?

Margot Your curtain call—your bow.

Leo No.

Margot Please. For me. As a birthday treat.

Leo No.

Margot Go on. I want to see your smile.

Leo Well…

Margot Hang on… (*Sighting the telescope or opera glasses*) Over there. OK. Do it over there.

Leo approaches her across the room and bows graciously

Leo There.

Margot Ghastly. Why so solemn?

Leo It was not solemn. I was smiling.

Margot Wincing. You looked all constipated and po-faced.

Leo Well, perhaps I've been playing *King Lear*.

Margot Well, pretend you're doing *Charley's Aunt*. Do that trotting thing you used to do, that was very engaging.

Leo Trotting?

Margot You used to sort of trot down to the footlights.

Leo I never trotted.

Margot You did. You trotted…

Leo I strode. I never trotted.

Margot Well, trot for me. Do it again.

Leo It's not appropriate. In my position one needs a little gravitas. I have got a K, remember.

Margot So it's the knighthood that's making you wince.
Leo It's not a bloody wince. It's a dignified, if thin, smile.
Margot You delude yourself. It's nothing short of a grimace.
Leo All right then, clever clogs. You do it. Let's see you take a damn bow.
Margot (*getting up*) What show have I been doing, then?
Leo *The Wreck of the Hesperus.*

Margot, not without pleasure, executes a charming bow/curtsy

Well, I have to admit that was charming. Warm and gracious, even a tad
coy perhaps. Shall we do one together?
Margot All right.
Leo As Romeo and Juliet?
Margot Why not?

*They do a very nice curtain call together, bowing to one another and then to
the audience. Leo kisses Margot's hand*

Leo I can't believe you're seventy. You look magnificent. You know at the
end of the day you and I are two of a kind. Sometimes I think to myself to
hell with it, the Hollywood crap, the salads and the hype and the whole
bogus shebang of it. All I really want is to be on some terrace in the South
of France, with the sun setting on the sea in front of me and a great wall of
bougainvillea behind me. A glass of Pouilly Fuissé in my hand and you
beside me playing backgammon in a dotty old hat.
Margot You are so full of shit.
Leo Thank you.
Margot And your teeth look just dandy. A bit like Burt Lancaster. So what
are you doing here?
Leo I came to see you.
Margot Oh yeah?
Leo Why should I lie?
Margot I don't know, you always like to keep in practice.
Leo You haven't changed at all.
Margot My case rests.

Sadie enters

Sadie I hope I'm not interrupting again.
Margot Not at all, Sadie. Sadie Croft, this is Leo Buchanan...
Leo How do you do?
Sadie (*shaking his hand*) How do you do? I'm so thrilled to meet you.
Leo Thank you.
Sadie I've always been a great fan of yours.

Margot Sadie is going to play Juliet, Leo, she came to ask for some advice. She's been reading P. J. Monckton's book.

Leo Oh, really? He is just a poncy old windbag with his head up his arse. That stuff about palpable heat. All this endless analysing of things, I don't believe in it.

Margot Unless of course you're on the Michael Parkinson show, then you get your head up your arse as quick as you can.

Leo Exactly. It's every man for himself.

Margot "Defend the galaxy with pride, kiddo".

Leo A good actor has to be as sly as a fox. He's not going to give away any real secrets, is he?

Margot Not with the man from the *News of the World* sitting on the front lawn with a black eye and his wife in the bar with a meat cleaver.

Sadie I suppose not. I mean, he even wanted to talk to me.

Leo Did he?

Sadie Asking all kinds of questions.

Leo Was he? How awful. Thank God no-one knows I'm here, eh?

Margot (*to Sadie*) Leo has a life-long habit of being caught with his pants down.

Leo She means figuratively.

Margot I meant literally.

Sadie No wonder you're in trouble, then.

Leo laughs a little nervously. The awkwardness is now palpable. Margot eyes them both through her telescope or opera glasses

Margot So how long has this been going on?

Sadie What do you mean?

Leo She knows.

Sadie Knows what? What does she know?

Margot I know.

Sadie What do you mean? What do you know?

Margot I know you're wearing Ysatis which is Leo's favourite scent, I know that aquamarine ring you're wearing probably has something Welsh inscribed on the inside. And I know what a sucker I've been.

Leo Margot, I'm so sorry.

Margot I don't like being taken for an idiot.

Leo It's not how it looks, I promise.

Margot Don't do that. Don't promise, Leo, it always means you're lying.

Sadie You must think I'm a right cow coming here?

Margot Yes. That sort of covers it.

Leo This wasn't planned, Margot—I'd no idea Sadie would be here.

Sadie Me neither.

Margot Having been there the last time you were caught cheating on your wife, in the leading role, it's all rather *déjà vu* for me. Are you really playing Juliet?

Sadie Oh, yes, of course. It was Leo's idea to write to you—he said you were the best person to talk to.

Margot Oh, did he? You don't think you might have mentioned it earlier, that you were shacked up with Mr Sly-As-A-Fox here.

Sadie To tell the truth, I very nearly did.

Leo I don't care much for "shacked up with"—we have an understanding.

Sadie We're in love.

Margot Aah. Is that right?

Leo More or less.

Margot More or less. That's hardly unequivocal, Leo. Would I be right in thinking that your wife doesn't know about this?

Leo No, not exactly.

Margot She has no understanding about your understanding.

Sadie You haven't told her.

Margot Me?

Sadie Her. Your wife.

Leo What?

Margot She means the other one. The title holder.

Leo No.

Sadie You haven't told her.

Leo I haven't had a chance.

Margot Oh my God. (*About to call for Mrs Kidd*) Let's get her in here and sort it out...

Leo I just need a little time. Things have got a bit on top of me.

Sadie You promised, Leo, you promised you'd tell her.

Margot Reading about it in the *News of the World* should help soften the blow for her.

Leo Margot, we don't need your snide little jokes.

Sadie You said it was all over. You said things hadn't been right between you for ages.

Leo They haven't. She just hasn't noticed. She's been very busy in the garden and things.

Sadie You said you were going to tell her. Get it out in the open.

Leo She's not like that. She's not a-let's-sit-round-the-kitchen-table-and-talk-this-through kind of person.

Margot More of a wrap-this-rolling-pin-round-your-head kind of person.

Leo Margot, please. (*Cajoling Sadie*) Sadie, be patient. Hmm? I'm under a lot of pressure.

Sadie What about the cottage?

Margot Cottage?

Sadie We found this wonderful little cottage just north of Banbury.

Margot Oh my God, not the dinky cottage with the wistaria round the porch. This is more serious than I thought.
Leo Clematis actually.

Sadie's mobile rings in her pocket or bag. She answers

Sadie (*into her mobile*) Hallo? ... Who? ... Graham Latimer? What's——
Margot (*to Leo, aside*) Have you ever seen *The Jerry Springer Show*? No? This is a bit like that.
Sadie (*into her mobile*) I've got nothing to tell you. (*Not into the phone*) He says he's outside... (*She goes to the window to see if she can see Graham Latimer*) Is that him with the red hair? (*Into the phone*) I'm here to see Margot Buchanan. ... Did she? (*To Margot*) He says you called him a scumbag.
Margot I heard it on *Brookside*.
Sadie Sir Leo? ... I've no idea. ... What? ... *How* much?
Leo Oh my God. What are they after?
Margot Some hints on home management perhaps.
Sadie (*covering the mouthpiece*) He's offering me a fortune if I can tell him anything.
Margot What's it called—like "shake 'n' vac" and "park 'n' ride" only with newspapers.
Leo Kiss 'n' tell.
Sadie Yes.
Leo You mustn't.
Sadie What?
Leo Kiss or tell.
Sadie Mustn't I?
Leo I'd deny it. There's no proof.
Sadie You snake. (*She puts down the mobile and empties her shoulder bag on to the table. Bundles of letters and stuff. She picks up one of those concertina strips of photographs*) In colour. *And* all your letters. (*Into her mobile*) Hold on a minute.
Leo Hang up, for God's sake, Sadie, let's talk about this. What the hell are you doing with all that stuff in your bag anyway?
Sadie Trying to save your skin, actually. My flatmate is a cousin of Nigel Dempster.
Leo Look, now is not the moment to go public.
Margot Isn't that a stock market thing? How much is he offering?

Judy enters, very composed

Judy Ah, there you are.
Leo Yes, here I am.

Margot There he is.

Sadie (*into the mobile*) I'll call you back. (*She disconnects*)

Margot There we are. Bingo. Doesn't this give me a full house?

Leo (*kissing Judy*) Hallo, darling.

Judy Fancy seeing you here.

Leo I just popped in to wish Margot Happy Birthday.

Judy Me too. I expect she was more gracious with you.

Margot Not a lot.

Leo What fuss and nonsense, eh? What a palaver. Reporters. Huh. What do they know?

Judy You tell me. (*She picks up the trailing strip of photographs*) Oh, look, what's all this, then?

Sadie They're mine.

Leo (*meaning Margot*) They're hers.

Margot They're mine. (*She scoops them up*)

Judy (*to Sadie*) You've met my husband, then, have you?

Sadie Yes.

Judy That was lucky for you.

Sadie What?

Judy A little bonus.

Sadie I beg your pardon?

Judy He played Romeo, didn't you, Leo?

Sadie Oh, yes. Yes, of course.

Judy In his youth. A long time ago. He's always been very keen on helping young aspirants, haven't you, Leo?

Leo (*modestly*) I do what I can.

Sadie Would that be with or without your head up your arse?

Judy What did you say?

Margot We were just talking about the mystery of acting.

Sadie How two people can create palpable heat together.

Judy Jolly tricky, I should imagine.

Leo It's a... It's not easy ... is it?

Judy (*taking Leo's arm*) Shall we go and talk to that chap on the lawn? Sort things out.

Leo Graham Latimer.

Judy He's been overdoing it a bit.

Sadie Burning his candle at both ends? That can be such a mistake.

Leo Well, it all depends ... doesn't it?

Judy On what?

Margot On the length of the candle.

Sadie Aren't you curious to know what's going on, Lady Buchanan?

Margot No, she isn't. Why don't you all go home?

Judy How exactly do you mean?

Leo (*to Sadie*) Tell you what, I'll give you a call some time and maybe we can do some work on your Juliet. Hmm?

A man dressed as Superman comes on. His costume is hopeless and his English is not good either

Superman Hallo. Big kiss for a lady—Buchanan. Which one that? I no kiss all.
Judy Who is this? Get him out of here.
Margot You were cancelled.
Superman Superman approaches. He kisses big. He kisses wet.
Leo Get the hell out of here.
Superman (*producing paperwork*) I have docket for kissing. Look.
Sadie You are not wanted.
Superman I am obliged to do kissing big wet. Kiss kiss. Yes?
Margot No. Kiss kiss yes is the last thing any of us need at this precise moment.

Mrs Kidd enters to sort things out

Mrs Kidd Now look here, Superman. You were cancelled.
Superman Eh? I have docket for kissing.
Mrs Kidd (*seeing him off to the garden*) Terminated. Not wanted. Go home.
Superman (*recognizing Leo*) Hey, you Sheriff of the Universe. "Defend galaxy with pride, kiddo"... You not proper agency kisser. You cheating kisser.
Margot You can say that again.
Superman You big bastard.

Mrs Kidd frog-marches Superman off into the garden

Margot All I wanted was a quiet birthday and what do I get? A sci-fi armageddon.
Leo Well, we'd better be going, hadn't we? Come along, darling.
Sadie Hang on a minute.
Judy Not so fast. Where were we?
Sadie Tell her.
Leo No.
Judy Oh yes, I remember. Tell me what?
Margot Tell her, for God's sake.
Leo Shut up, Margot. It's none of your business.
Margot I live here—it's my birthday.
Leo This is neither the time nor the place.

Sadie It's not a question of time or place.
Judy Leo. Leo, what is all this about?
Sadie It's about us.
Judy Us. You and him?
Sadie Yes.
Judy You and my husband?
Sadie That's it.
Judy Leo—what is she saying? Tell me she's not telling me something is
   going on between you two.
Leo I can't.
Judy What?
Leo I can't tell you she's not telling you that.
Judy You mean you're having an affair with this girl?
Leo Yes.
Judy Behind my back?
Leo Yes.
Judy I don't believe it. Under my nose?
Margot You can't have it both ways.
Judy What?
Margot It can't be behind your back *and* under your nose.
Judy Shut up.
Margot How dare you talk to me like that.
Judy I want an explanation, Leo. And I want it now.
Margot It's perfectly simple—he came, he kissed big and wet and now he's
   up a gum tree, poor old sausage.
Judy (*to Leo*) Is this true?

*Sadie's mobile rings and Sadie holds it out towards Leo, the mobile still
ringing*

Sadie Well?
Leo Hang on a minute.
Judy Leo.
Leo Look, let's all keep calm.
Sadie (*into the mobile*) Hallo. ... Yes, it is... (*To the others*) It's Graham
   Latimer.
Leo Hang up. Hang up. (*He snatches the mobile. Sweetly*) Hi, Graham. ...
   No, everything is fine. A little birthday party, that's all. ... Try putting some
   arnica on it... Bye. (*He disconnects and puts Sadie's mobile in his pocket*)
   Look, I know I've made a bit of a balls up of things here, I've been under
   a lot of pressure and stuff, but we've all just got to sit down and work it
   out...
Judy (*standing up*) I'm not bloody well sitting down...
Leo (*to Judy*) It's all over, I tell you...

Sadie You bastard…
Leo (*to Sadie*) I need time. Give me a break, Sadie…
Judy You bastard.
Leo Margot—for God's sake… Please.
Margot No, I'm afraid I'm with them. We're unanimous. You're a bastard.

Leo gasps with pain and falls to the ground, clutching his chest. The mobile starts to ring again

Judy Leo. Leo. What are you playing at?
Margot What's happening?
Sadie It's Leo. He's fainted. Loosen his tie.
Judy You shut up. He's pretending.
Margot Put his head between his knees. Ring the bell.
Judy Leo. Leo is this for real? Leo? Leo, pull yourself… Oh my God.

Mrs Kidd enters

Mrs Kidd What is all this noise. (*Seeing the situation*) Stand back, everybody… (*She gets busy doing her life-saving stuff*) Well, let's see what we've got here. Stand back, would you, Lady Buchanan. (*She takes Leo's pulse*) Now… Has he had any heart problems? Is he on any pills?

Superman enters from the garden

Superman Agency rule—"no kiss no pay". I kiss someone very quickly and go. Yes?
The Others No. Go away. Get out of here. Take him away. (*Etc.*)

Freda enters from the hall. She is seeing an apparition

Superman (*to Freda*) You lady, I kiss you big wet. Yes?
Freda (*to her invisible apparition*) No, no, no, no…

Chaos. The Lights fade

CURTAIN

ACT II

A few minutes later

An inert substitute of Leo's body is on a stretcher and partially hidden from view

Judy, Margot and Sadie are clustered round, watching Mrs Kidd trying to revive the body on the floor. Freda is prowling about in pursuit of an invisible something

The Lights fade up slowly

Judy Anything? Any flicker?
Mrs Kidd I can't tell.
Margot Keep trying. Carry on.
Freda (*shooing*) No, no, no. Go on, get back. Get back.
Margot Freda, darling, calm down.
Sadie Give his chest another thump.

The Lights are now fully up as Mrs Kidd mightily thumps the corpse's chest

    Leo emerges among them. All his black clothing is now white. He is a ghost and we quickly realize he is visible and audible only to Freda and to us

Leo Ow! What the hell is going on?
Freda (*very anxiously*) Go away. Get back.
Leo What?
Freda (*pointing to his body*) In there. Into your body. Go on.
Sadie Miss Deacon, do be quiet.

Mrs Kidd thumps the chest of the corpse hard. Leo reels

Leo What on earth does that woman think she is doing?
Judy Any luck?
Mrs Kidd I don't think so.
Sadie Do it again.
Leo No, no, don't.
Freda (*leading him out of earshot*) She is trying to save your life.

Leo My life?
Freda That's you there on the stretcher, you are fighting for your life. You've
  had a heart attack.
Leo You mean I'm... Oh, dear, that's awful.

*Mrs Kidd gives the corpse a kiss of life. Leo looks on appalled. He reacts to
her breath*

  My God what has this woman been eating?

*Another huge thump from Mrs Kidd. Possibly the hovering between life and
the other thing*

  (*Wavering*) Ah... Aaaaaaaaah.
Mrs Kidd Come on, come on.
Judy Was there something?
Mrs Kidd A flutter, I think.
Leo A flutter? It was like a sledge hammer.
Margot Try again. Go on.
Judy Yes, yes, keep trying.

Another thump

Leo Aaaaah. I'm an actor not a sumo bloody wrestler.
Sadie Well?
Mrs Kidd Nothing, I'm afraid.
Judy Oh my God.
Mrs Kidd He's gone. I'm so sorry, Lady Buchanan.

*The three women silently take in their grief. Leo takes a look at himself and
then talks to Freda confidentially*

Leo Is that it?
Freda I'm afraid it is.
Leo I'm dead.
Freda Yes.
Leo Bloody hell.
Freda That'll come later, I expect.
Leo So that's what it was.
Freda What?
Leo I had this God-awful pain in my chest and then...
Freda Oh, do tell. I do so want to know what it's like, the crossing.
Margot Freda, darling, sssh, poor Leo has gone.
Leo Gone... Gone. I'm here.

Freda shakes her head vehemently and points

That's me, is it, my corpse? (*He looks at his body*) I do look a bit peaky, I must say.

Sadie I can't believe it. I can't believe it.

Leo Neither can I. There's never been anything wrong with my heart. There must be some mistake.

Judy (*to the body*) Oh my darling, oh my poor Leo.

Leo Dead. I can't be dead. I'm supposed to be doing *Ready Steady Cook* on Thursday.

Freda You are dead. Finito. Terminado. Amen.

Margot For God's sake, Freda.

Mrs Kidd Miss Deacon, why don't you go and sit down.

Leo (*outraged*) I can't be dead. Tell me it's not true.

Freda is not going to risk speaking, she mimes that Leo is dead with the cutting-of-the-throat gesture and then drops her head in a dead fashion

Well, what happened to the bit where your whole life flashes before your eyes, I never had that. All I got was a ghastly little foreigner in red tights.

Mrs Kidd I think that's the doctor arriving. (*She makes for the exit*) I think it would be best if we moved him into the surgery…

Mrs Kidd exits

Margot sits lost in her thoughts, Judy sobs quietly over the body and Sadie paces about trying to take it all in. Freda goes to her chair US. *Leo is stunned*

Leo This is ridiculous. (*Loudly*) Hallo. Hallo. Look, everybody, I'm here. (*He dances about*) It's all right. No need for tears…

None of them see him even when he waves his arms about, etc.

Coooooooeeeeee.

Freda (*quietly*) They can't see you or hear you.

Leo Oh dear, oh dear. That's terrible. (*He goes to Judy and pats her gently*)

She reacts as if to a cold draught. He goes to comfort Sadie with a little squeeze and she jumps as if electrocuted. Freda urgently takes him aside

Freda (*confidentially*) No, no, no. You mustn't do that. No touching. No stunts. No practical jokes.

Leo What? Why not?

Freda It's just not done. It's considered very bad form. People are so easily spooked.

Leo You mean I'm a... I can't be a...

Freda Actually we never use the word.

Leo What word?

Freda (*a little too loudly*) Ghost. Ghost.

Margot Not now, Freda. Put your headset on.

Freda Sorry. (*To Leo*) You see.

Sadie He wasn't that old.

Judy Only sixty-eight.

Margot Seventy-one actually.

Judy Sixty-eight on his passport.

Margot Maybe, but seventy-one on his birth certificate.

Judy I'm telling you he was sixty-eight.

Margot Seventy-one.

Judy Sixty-eight.

Margot Fifty quid says he's seventy-one.

Leo (*to Judy, unheard of course*) Don't take it.

Judy I don't think so.

Margot They made him lop off three years when he was a child star and when he got his scholarship to RADA he kind of forgot to put them back.

Sadie He told *me* he was only fifty-nine.

Judy You keep your nose out of this. (*To the corpse*) Seventy-one, eh? You never told me about that, did you?

Leo What does it matter? I'm not telling everyone about your liposuction in High Wycombe last year.

Again the three women fall into a sad silence

Judy He was a dear man, a dear dear man.

Margot Yes, he was. In his way. A dear man.

Sadie A dear man.

Leo At least you're all agreed on that. Twenty minutes ago you were all calling me a bastard.

Margot I... er... I'm sorry if I was unpleasant earlier, Lady Buch... Judy... I shouldn't have been so ... so...

Judy Cantankerous.

Margot Exactly. I'm sorry. Really, I am.

Judy Poor darling, he was not good at handling stress.

Margot No, although God knows he created enough of it.

Judy I kept telling him to take up golf. But he always said...

Leo ⎫
　　　 ⎬ (*together*) I hate golf and what's more I hate bloody golfers.
Judy ⎭

Silence again. Leo takes another look at himself

Leo (*to Freda*) I think she might have been right about those teeth. I don't
   look at all good. Freda, do you think you could close my mouth for me, I
   don't want anyone seeing me like that... Please.

*Reluctantly, Freda agrees and quietly (unnoticed) sets about the task of
shutting the corpse's mouth*

Judy I got him that suit last year in New York.
Sadie Why did he always wear black?
Margot To hide his waistline.
Leo Steady on.
Judy And of course his sense of colour wasn't that good.
Margot Quite dreadful.
Sadie Ghastly.
Margot You keep out of it.
Judy It's funny, isn't it, he always said he'd rather go with a bang than a
   whimper...
Leo Yes, but not now. Not in my prime.
Sadie Thank God he didn't suffer anyway.
Leo I had the hell thumped out of me by old Mrs Dog Breath.
Margot It was certainly quick.
Sadie Yes, it was certainly quick.
Judy You mind your own business.
Leo Please don't anyone say it's what he would have wanted.
Judy He wouldn't have liked a lingering sort of thing.
Leo I would, I could have done with a bit of lingering as it happens.
Margot He wasn't good at being ill, if I remember. Even back in the Sixties
   he made a terrible fuss about his sinuses.
Leo It turned out to be a wisdom tooth.
Freda That can be horrid.
Leo Thank you.
Judy No, he always got very grumpy when he was ill. I mean even last year
   when he had a bit of trouble with his...
Leo Oh no, no, no, no. Not that.
Margot What?
Judy Men's problem. You know with his undercarriage.
Margot He had problems with his undercarriage, did he? (*To herself*) So
   there is a God after all.
Judy He was very irascible, poor poppet. Especially when...
Leo Freda, for God's sake stop them...
Freda (*loudly to the corpse*) Will you be quiet...

They all turn and watch in horror as Freda is busily fiddling with the corpse's mouth

You stupid stupid man.

Margot (*kindly*) Freda, darling, Leo's dead.

Freda Of course he's dead, I know that.

Margot Then what are you doing?

Freda I thought he might be happier with his mouth shut, I'm just trying to close it.

Judy I think you should leave him alone.

Leo Carry on. Carry on.

Margot (*with her telescope or opera glasses*) Actually he does look rather gormless.

Freda He's gone a bit stiff.

Sadie It can't be rigor mortis already?

Freda Oh my God.

Margot What is it?

Freda Nothing.

Judy What have you got there?

Freda Nothing.

Judy Show me what's in your hand.

Freda (*holding up Leo's teeth*) I'm so sorry.

Margot What is it?

Judy His teeth.

Freda They just came out.

Leo Bloody well put them back.

Judy Put them back.

Freda I can't, his jaw has gone all rigid.

Sadie Oh, for Heaven's sake.

They all stoop over the body, trying to replace the teeth

Margot Leave them out. Who cares?

Leo I do, I look like Boris Karloff.

Margot The undertaker will sort it out.

Leo (*panicked*) Undertaker. They'll take me to an undertaker?

Freda nods

Oh, no, this is unbearable. Freda, you must tell them I don't want embalming. I don't want a lot of greasy little nerds jamming putty up my orifices.

Freda I'll do my best.

Leo I had a dresser once in Darlington who claimed he was a reflexologist, that was bad enough.

Sadie He's all cold.

Judy Get your hands off him.

Mrs Kidd enters with two staff members, Robin and Francis, in white coats (played by ASMs)

Mrs Kidd For goodness sake, what are you all doing?

Judy We're trying to get his teeth back in.

Mrs Kidd How did they come out?

Margot Don't ask.

Sadie (*succeeding with the teeth*) There we are.

Leo (*looking at himself*) Oh my God.

Mrs Kidd Er... Aren't they supposed to be in the upper jaw.

Leo Of course they are, I look like a gerbil.

Mrs Kidd We'll sort it out later, shall we? That's right, Robin, you take this end ... we'll just take him through to the surgery. Lady Buchanan, perhaps you'd like to come with us?

Judy Thank you.

A mobile phone starts ringing. They are leaving with the stretcher. Everybody looks about. At last it is clear that the mobile is on the corpse. Judy and Mrs Kidd empty all his pockets

Sadie That's my mobile... It's in his pocket.

Mrs Kidd In his jacket perhaps.

Judy (*pocketing a wad of money*) I'll look after that ... what's this?

Leo Oh ... my ... God.

Mrs Kidd (*putting it on the tray*) It's a packet of condoms, Lady Buchanan.

Judy (*scrutinising it*) I don't believe it. Strawberry flavoured.

Mrs Kidd (*finding the ringing mobile*) Here we are.

Judy (*into the mobile*) Hallo. Hallo? ... Who? ... Graham Latimer? ... No, it isn't Sadie Croft. This is Lady Buchanan. ... Yes, I am. ... No, we have no plans to separate. Everything is fine between us. Fine. ... Yes, a little misunderstanding, that's all. A storm in a teacup. ... Yes, he's a little ... under the weather. ... Yes, right beside me. ... No, he doesn't want to talk to you just now. He's...

Leo Busy.

Freda Busy.

Judy Busy. He's busy. (*She looks at the corpse*) Hm? ... Well, he says, try putting a raw steak on it, and no hard feelings. Goodbye. (*She hangs up and looks round at her spectators sheepishly*)

Leo Poor old Graham Latimer, he'll be in for a bit of a bollocking from his Editor.

Judy (*to the dead Leo, regarding the condoms*) What about these, then?

Freda What are they?

Leo ⎫ (*together*) French letters.
Margot ⎭

Leo Damn things—nothing but trouble.

Judy (*fondly to the stiff*) An empty flask, half a bar of chocolate and a packet of three strawberry-flavoured Earth Movers. Why don't you grow up?

Leo A bit late for that.

Mrs Kidd Shall we go?

The body is borne off by the two staff members and followed by Mrs Kidd

Judy waits a moment

Leo Am I supposed to go with me or what?

Freda I've no idea.

Leo I don't have to clear customs or anything?

Freda Sssssh. Be quiet.

Judy (*to Sadie*) I don't want to seem vindictive, Miss...

Sadie Croft.

Judy I don't know exactly what your relationship was with my husband, I don't want to know, but as far as I'm concerned it's wiped from the record. You have no claim against Leo. None whatever.

Sadie Is that all?

Judy I never want to see or hear from you again, not through the post, not in the press, not at all. Do I make myself clear?

Sadie Perfectly clear. I just want to say... I didn't want to fall in love with him, you know, your husband.

Margot None of us bloody well did.

Leo Girls, please, I want a good clean fight.

Sadie You know, it wasn't guilt I felt about you, Lady Buchanan, it was just compassion, sympathy from one woman to another...

Judy I wasn't actually looking for sistership, Miss Croft. (*She throws the condoms at her*) And you know where you can put those.

Judy exits

Sadie Well, that was nice.

Leo Please, Freda, tell them I'm here. Please, please, help me.

Freda (*loudly*) No, no, no.

Margot (*comforting Freda*) I know it's hard to take in, isn't it, darling?

Leo They are distraught, poor darlings. How are they going to cope without me?

Freda (*flaring up*) You are the most conceited egotistical bastard.

Margot Don't tell me you've got Leo's ghost there already.

Leo Show some respect. (*To Freda*) Go on, tell them. Please.

Freda Actually, Margot... Supposing I told you that Leo *is* here, right there in front of you as a matter of fact.

Leo And I'm absolutely fine.

Freda And he's absolutely fine.

Leo does a little bit of flamenco dancing to prove his point

He's doing a bit of flamenco.

Margot Have another pill, darling. Put your headphones on.

Freda (*to Leo*) You see. (*To the others*) What I don't understand, though, is why do those things have to be strawberry-flavoured?

Sadie I can't explain.

Margot Leo never liked strawberries anyway. Raspberries, yes, and loganberries. Don't they do raspberries?

Freda You can't beat a good gooseberry in my book.

Sadie Can we change the subject?

Freda Well, how come there's only one left?

Sadie He was a bit tired, actually.

Leo (*outraged*) I was not.

Freda I was a dutch cap girl myself.

Margot Gin and tonic flavoured, I suppose.

Leo I don't bloody well believe this, there am I being carted off to the morgue and they're reminiscing about birth control.

Sadie goes and stares out of the window and Margot reaches down, feeling for the box of Kleenex, not finding it, she tries the other side. Leo very gently moves the box with his foot so that she can take a tissue. She is slightly disturbed by the event. Sadie comes over to her

Sadie Are you OK?

Margot Not altogether.

Sadie Me neither. I just want to say I'm sorry I deceived you. I should have told you straight away what was going on.

Margot It's none of my business.

Sadie You're not cross or jealous or anything?

Margot Good Lord, no. Well, only a bit. I mean, if someone writes off your car that's upsetting, isn't it? But if you sell your car to someone and then he writes it off—that's not quite so bad.

Leo So now I'm an old banger.

Sadie But you still feel something for him?

Margot Irritation mostly.

Leo Aaaaah.

Margot I remember the first time I saw him. It was the first rehearsal of *Romeo and Juliet*...

Leo At the stage door of the *Globe*.

Margot At the stage door of the *Globe*. He drew up in his old Morris.

Leo (*to Freda, who is listening*) A bullnosed Morris.

Margot And he wound down the window... (*She chuckles*) And he was wearing this perfectly ghastly cravat, I mean awful...

Leo Rather nice—sort of yellow paisley actually...

Margot And he stuck out his hand and he said...

Leo ⎱ (*together; not quite in unison*) "Leo Buchanan. You must be
Margot ⎰ playing the Nurse"...

Margot The Nurse. I ask you.

Sadie So it was love at first sight, was it?

Margot Not quite, it was a couple of weeks before I got the full-blown symptoms...

Leo Me too.

Margot He made me feel everything I wanted to be, witty, intelligent, talented, beautiful. He even said I had Botticelli feet. (*She waggles her foot*) You wouldn't think it, would you?

Leo Not now, of course, you daft old thing.

Sadie So all this was going on, was it, all through rehearsals?

Margot Yup. It was cooking along. Oh dear, oh dear ... you see we had this deal...

Leo No. Stop. Not that. That's private. Freda, tell her...

Freda Sssssh. (*To Margot*) Carry on, Margot. What was this deal?

Margot We agreed not to do it, not to go the whole hog, you know, the full fandango until after the play had opened... (*A bit of reverie*)

Sadie Wow.

Freda Go on. Go on.

Leo No, no, don't.

Margot Yes, well, anyway, we blew it...

Sadie The deal?

Margot Yes.

Sadie No.

Margot (*laughing like a girl*) In the interval... On the first night.

They all laugh

In my dressing room. What a business, with all the petticoats and tights and his codpiece and things. He was a real rogue...

Leo What do you mean?

Margot ...There was no stopping him.

Leo It was all *your* idea.

Sadie Hence the "palpable heat" that Monckton was on about. So he was your first love, was he?

Margot My first, yes, but not my only, not by a long long chalk.

Leo Not too long, I hope.

Sadie What about him?

Margot Leo? (*She chuckles*) Was I his first love?... No. He lost his virginity at RADA. Bless him.

Leo (*chuckling to Freda*) Yes, siree, bob. What a way to spend a wet afternoon.

Sadie With a fellow student, you mean?

Margot No, the traditional older woman, the elocution teacher in the second year. They all called her ... what was it?

Leo The raven-haired bicycle made for two...

Margot (*remembering, not hearing*) The raven-haired bicycle made for two ... a real nympho. Apparently they all had her.

Leo (*to Freda*) She was one hell of a woman.

Freda puts her headset on again

Margot He was always a darling man really, one of those rogues who says "I love you" just when a decent man would say "I'll call you a taxi". How about you, how are you doing?

Sadie I don't really know what I feel.

Leo Bereft? Devastated?

Sadie I mean I was in love with him, of course. But I suppose if I'm honest...

Leo Please don't be. We don't need honesty at this point.

Sadie I wasn't really that confident that we had a future together. Not long term. I mean there is a hell of an age gap.

Leo You always said it never bothered you.

Sadie I always said it never bothered me, of course.

Margot You can't have had that much in common.

Leo We had plenty.

Sadie Exactly. I mean his idea of fun was a picnic at Glynebourne, cold grouse and claret.

Margot Lovely. With fresh asparagus?

Leo Oh, yes, and then a bit of Stilton...

Margot And then a bit of Stilton followed by raspberries and cream...

Leo Raspberries and cream—perfect.

Sadie He was always telling me what fun the two of you had together.

Margot Was he? Yes, we had some good times.

Sadie But despite all the denial, I suppose I do have to admit he was a father figure.

Leo Oh no ... that is just pitiful.

Sadie Although actually he was quite sexy.

Leo That's better.

Margot (*laughing*) Especially after lunch if I remember.

Sadie (*laughing*) Especially after lunch. Him and his games.

Margot He wasn't still up to all that fantasy stuff, was he?

Sadie (*as a french maid*) Mais oui, monsieur, à vôtre service. (*Wistfully*) Poor old Mr Woodpecker.

Margot What did you say?

Sadie Mr Woodpecker. It was just a silly name we used to use.

Margot (*a little put out*) Oh, was it? Well, that's very original.

Leo (*to his trouser front*) You see the trouble you cause me.

Margot So what do you reckon you'll do now?

Sadie You mean now as in henceforward? I've no idea. It all looks a bit bleak. I mean, he really had promised me he'd get everything sorted out. Oh God. (*She reaches for the Kleenex*)

Leo again dextrously moves the box for her benefit. She blows her sad nose

Leo My poor darling—chin up.

Sadie I mean it's all right for her, the official widow, but I'm left with nothing. Sweet F. A.

Leo Try and be brave.

Sadie (*she blows her nose*) Except all those letters and stuff.

Leo Not too brave.

Margot What? You mean sell them to what's-his-name out there with the red hair?

Leo paces about the room in consternation

Sadie Graham Latimer. I mean, I don't owe that cow anything.

Margot No, indeed, none of us do.

Leo (*to Freda*) Please, you must help me, you must interrupt them. I'm in deep trouble.

Freda (*loudly*) Sod off.

Margot Sod off yourself.

Sadie I mean, why shouldn't the world know that we were an item.

Leo For God's sake. Please tell her not to.

Freda (*giving him the finger*) No.

Margot I wonder how the old boy would feel about being besmirched now he's...

Leo unplugs Freda's headphones and turns the radio up loud

(*To Freda*) What are you doing?
Freda (*dancing*) I just felt like a bit of a dance.

Leo snatches Freda's hat off her head or from her table and throws it across the room. Margo and Sadie are surprised

Margot What was that?
Freda My hat.
Sadie What are you doing?
Freda I never liked it.

Sadie gives it back to her

Thank you. Why don't you two go and have a drink? In the bar. (*She plugs in the headphones*)
Margot (*rising*) Good idea. (*To Sadie*) She's probably got one of her visitors.
Leo She has. She has.
Sadie You mean a ghost?
Freda Good Lord, no. Anyway, Margot's a D.B.I.G. person.
Sadie What's that?
Freda A Don't Believe In Ghosts person.
Margot I just can't bear the thought of the dear departed wafting about in white sheets going "whoooo whoooo".

For a moment Margot and Leo whoo-whooo directly to one another

Then Sadie and Margot exit together

Leo At last we can talk properly.
Freda No, we can't. I want you to go away.
Leo You mean my body? You don't mean me, the spirit.
Freda Both. (*She looks down the passage*) Actually, you the body are being carted off to the morgue even as we speak.
Leo (*watching, very sad*) That's me... Oh, my God... Farewell, old friend... Do you suppose I'll be able to go to my funeral?
Freda I think that would be rather common, actually.
Leo I'll just have to watch it on telly.
Freda On telly? They're not going to have your funeral on telly.
Leo They might if the racing is cancelled. By the way, could you mention to someone I'd like to have *For Those in Peril on the Sea*.
Freda I'm not a disc jockey, for goodness sake.

Leo I really need your help, Freda. I'm desperate to straighten things out with my poor darling girls.

Freda You don't think that in mortal terms you've left it a bit late for that?

Leo I've got to find a way of persuading Sadie not to sell this stuff. I mean, I don't mind all the disgrace but it doesn't seem fair on everyone else... Judy, my daughter... Oh my God, little Rosalind... I'd just like a chance to redeem myself. Can't we do a deal? Hm? Surely there's something I could do for you?

Freda Like what? (*She moves to her jigsaw*)

Leo I don't know—I could spook your agent or pour hot tea over a theatre critic.

Freda (*at the jigsaw*) You seriously think I give a damn?

Leo You don't like me, is that it?

Freda No.

Leo No? No—just like that? No.

Freda All right then—no, *not at all*.

Leo Well, what have I ever done to you?

Freda It's of no importance... But if you really must know—there was a time long ago when I was down on my luck and I had to take the job of elocution teacher for the second year students at RADA.

Leo (*aghast*) Mrs Halliwell...

Freda (*nodding*) I was newly divorced and my hair was a lot darker in those days.

Leo Oh my God.

Freda Exactly. So when you ask if I like you, the raven-haired bicycle made for two replies, no, not at all.

Leo I never connected Freda Deacon with Mrs Halliwell... I thought you must be dead or in America or something.

Freda Rather nearer to death than America, I suppose. Now known to the residents here as The Ghostbuster. (*Moving him*) Mind your hand, I'm looking for a willy.

Leo It's good to see you after all this time... Small world, eh? What can I say?

Freda What can you say? You can say—"I'm sorry I never rang or wrote or even came to class again. You can say here's the 17/6 I owe you for the curry we had together in Potters Bar". Were you really a virgin, by the way?

Leo Sort of half.

Freda I thought they only did it in full sizes. Mr Woodpecker.

Leo (*chuckling*) Mr Woodpecker... Good Heavens... I've never been so embarrassed. I could die.

Freda You just did.

Leo I am so so sorry. (*With a piece*) Is this the willy you're after?

Freda Yes. So you can see I'm not overly keen to risk the funny farm just so that you can sort out all the mess you've left behind.

Leo sees the case he left in the conservatory when he first arrived. It gives him an idea

Leo Well, if not for me then for Margot.

Freda How do you mean?

Leo She's your friend.

Freda The only one I have left. The only one who doesn't mind me being barmy.

Leo Then let me talk to her at least.

Freda To what purpose?

Leo There's something I must do, something I have to give her. (*Indicating the parcel by his case*)

Freda It's too late. Too late. You've handed in your dinner plate…

Judy enters, puzzled: who is Freda talking to?

Judy Another "friend on the other side". Eh? (*She picks up Margot's telephone*) Mrs Kidd is putting me through to Rosalind. Our daughter.

Freda Would you like me to leave?

Leo She's in Australia. Cairns actually.

Freda (*very comforting*) Lovely… Do you want one of Margot's wine gums?

Judy No, thanks.

Freda (*putting her headset on*) Well, I'll just…

Leo Oh, Freda, what am I to do? I can't bear being dead. How can I have been such a complete bastard? I'm not sure I can handle it.

Freda "White Sole Lundy—visibility good to variable"…

Judy Ssshh. (*Into her phone*) Hallo. Rosalind, darling. It's Mummy. … I'm sorry. Is it? (*She checks her watch*) Sort of lunchtime. … Have you, my darling? How marvellous. … A shark? … No. That does sound fun. … Darling, is Amanda with you? … Good. Well, I'm sorry to wake her too. … Look, my darling, something awful, something really awful has happened. (*She paces about*) … No, my darling, not Dobbin. … Yes. Daddy. … Yes. … No, my darling, I'm afraid he's. … Yes. About an hour ago. A heart attack, we think… (*She looks at the spot*) He just collapsed. … Yes, I was. I was with him. … No, I don't think he did, it was very quick.

Leo Oh, my baby, my poor baby. My darlings.

Judy Yes, my darling, I wish you were too. … Yes, get hold of the travel people. … Yes. No, I'll pay this end. As soon as you can. Some time next week I suppose. I know it's impossible to take in, isn't it? So so sad. … Yes. Yes, he was.

Leo tries to listen in

Leo (*to Freda*) You see. I was.
Judy Very. ... Yes, wasn't he? Very. ... All right, my pet. Call me later—
at home. ... Yes. ... And me you, my darling... (*She disconnects*)

Leo is miserable

Mrs Kidd enters with a cup of tea

Mrs Kidd Your tea, Lady Buchanan. Did you get through all right?
Judy Yes, thank you. Poor darling, she's only eighteen. They were very
close.
Mrs Kidd Fathers and daughters—that's something special, isn't it?
Judy Yes, I suppose it is. I think I must have missed out on that.
Mrs Kidd I'm afraid we've had the press on the telephone.
Judy So soon?
Mrs Kidd Perhaps we should get your solicitor to draft a statement.
Leo And call my agent. She must call my agent.
Freda And his agent. You must call his agent.
Mrs Kidd Honestly, you actors, you're all the same.

Mrs Kidd and Judy exit

After a moment, Margot appears in the conservatory rather furtively

She taps the glass lightly

Margot Has she gone?

*Freda does not hear. Leo nudges Freda who is a little startled. A moment of
cross purposes*

Freda Yes.
Margot (*entering*) Good.
Freda Oh, hallo.
Leo Go on, please... Tell her I'm here.
Freda (*to Leo*) You are incorrigible.
Margot I can't help it, I just can't stand her.
Leo Go on. Go on. Please.
Freda Are you all right, darling? How are you doing?
Margot Not very well, I'm afraid. I mean, why does he have to come down
here to die? Right under my nose ... on my birthday. I mean, if he'd died
anywhere else—Hemel Hempstead or Honolulu—I could have held on to
the idea that he really didn't care about me.

Leo I did, I do, I do.

Freda I bet he did actually.

Margot (*a bit choked*) You'd think a woman of my age, in my state of decrepitude would know better than to let herself go giddy with pleasure at the sight of him.

Freda Even with those teeth?

Margot Yes—even with those teeth. It's funny, isn't it, how wrong men get it.

Leo nudges Freda for a response

Freda How do you mean?

Margot Leo never had the slightest idea why I loved him... He liked to think it was because he was handsome and sophisticated and sexy... The truth is he was actually quite an ordinary man...

Leo Ordinary? Me, ordinary?

Margot Kind and funny and gentle. Weak-willed, of course, and moody and indecisive and shambolic...

Leo Get her back on to the good bits.

Margot But a day hasn't gone by, not in all these years, when I haven't missed him like hell.

Freda wipes Margot's cheek, she is unaware of her tears

What are you doing?

Freda You've got mascara all down your stupid face.

Leo Oh, my darling... (*He points Freda to the parcel*) Freda. Please, please, please.

Freda (*reluctantly*) Er... Margot darling, I couldn't help but notice that there seems to be a parcel down here for you... (*She hands her the parcel*) Here.

Margot For me? (*She opens it with difficulty*) What can it be? Who is it from?

Freda There's a card. (*She takes it*) It just says: "I would I were thy bird".

Leo It's from the end of the balcony scene.

Freda It's from the end of the balcony scene.

Margot I know it's from the end of the balcony bloody scene. He is a dreadful old ham. (*She opens the parcel*) What the hell is it?...

Freda It's a painting.

Margot A painting?

Freda A portrait. Of a young girl sitting by a fountain...

Margot ...in a rose garden. Wearing a blue dress?

Leo Cornflower blue.

Margot A cornflower blue dress?

Freda Yes, exactly.

Margot Hold it up.

Freda holds it up. Margot studies it through her telescope or opera glasses

Back a bit… Just there. (*She stares at it*) So he was the anonymous buyer.
Freda (*looking at the painting*) Don't tell me that's you.
Margot It was. Fifty years ago.
Freda By Augustus John.
Margot Leo paid sixty-five thousand pounds for it. (*She laughs*) He had to
   buy it off himself, poor chap.
Freda Why would he do that?
Margot Because he didn't want his wife to know.
Leo I may be dead but I'm not stupid.
Margot I don't think I've ever been so touched.
Leo (*he is very close to Margot*) Nor me.
Freda I should imagine he's pretty touched too.
Margot (*suddenly sensing Leo a little*) Freda, you would tell me, wouldn't
   you—if you got anything?
Freda You mean from Leo—a message?
Margot Yes. Or if he turned up, you would tell me, wouldn't you?
Leo Go on. Please.
Freda Of course I would, but I just don't think he's the type. He's not ghost
   material.

Leo pinches Freda

Ow.
Margot What was that?
Freda Nothing.
Margot I mean, even a sort of sign would be nice.
Freda Like what?

*Leo picks up a vase of flowers and waltzes around with it in front of Margot,
going whoooo whoooo*

Margot Yes, something like that.
Freda (*flaring up involuntarily*) Don't do that, you stupid man, I told you
   no stunts. No tricks, OK?
Margot (*thrilled*) You've got him, haven't you? He's here.
Freda No. No… I'm not sure. It might be just a common or garden
   poltergeist.
Margot Well… Test him, then.
Freda How do you mean?

Margot Um... Ask him what happened ... on Guy Fawkes night in ... 1953. Go on.

Leo (*instantly remembering*) We had a bonfire party on Malibu beach and the police arrested me for burning an effigy, they thought it was a pagan ritual.

Margot Well? What's he say?

Freda (*frightened*) Er... He says, er ... you were ... on a camping holiday in Tunbridge Wells and you both got food poisoning.

Margot Oh. Are you sure? I've never been to Tunbridge Wells.

Freda Well, there you are then. False alarm. Isn't it nearly time for lunch?

Margot What was my private nickname for him then?

Leo Mr Woodpecker.

Freda (*involuntarily loudly*) Mr Woodpecker?

Margot Ah-ha. You *are* there. He is there.

Leo Geronimo!

Freda (*resigned*) Yes, he is. Bloody hell.

Margot Oh goodie goodie. How is he? How are you?

Leo Well, the actual death thing was a bit tricky, but I'm fine. Fine.

Freda He says the actual death thing was a bit tricky, but he's fine. Fine.

Margot Good. What's it like? Has he seen God?

Leo Not yet—just some ghastly Italian in red tights. Perhaps I'm in hell.

Freda I don't think he's even got to the Pearly Gates.

Margot Will you thank him, thank from the bottom of my heart for this... (*She indicates the painting*) He really is the sweetest man. (*She kisses the air nowhere near Leo*)

Freda He's over there actually.

Margot Oh. (*She blows a kiss*) You're an angel.

Leo I expect that will come later.

Margot (*shouting*) I can't tell you how pleased I am.

Freda He can hear you, there's no need to shout.

Leo Thank you. I'm very pleased you're pleased.

Freda He's very pleased you're pleased.

Margot So is it fun being a ghost? Can you float and things and pass through walls? I'd love to be able to do that. I could waft through the wall there and tie a knot in Emily Glover's catheter... Do tell me what it's like... How do you feel?

Leo Like Marcel Marceau in a darkened room.

Freda He says he feels like Marcel Marceau in a darkened room. This is ridiculous. Look, I really can't go on like this...

Margot Can't we communicate direct? He could give me a signal. Bang an ashtray or clink a glass.

Leo Good idea.

Freda No, no, no, absolutely not. That's just not on.

Leo bangs an ashtray loudly on the table

Margot Got you.
Freda Stop it. You can't do that sort of thing.
Leo Mind your own business.
Freda I could get you exorcized, then you'd be up shit creek without a
    paddle.
Margot Put your headset on, Freda.

Freda, thoroughly irritated, puts on her headset

  Right. One bang for yes. Two for no. OK?

Leo bangs the ashtray once

  Good. We have lift-off.

One bang

  Here we are then.

One bang

  I hated you dying.
Leo (*with one bang*) It wasn't much fun for me either.
Margot Does this mean I'm now one of your old haunts?

One bang

  That was a joke.

Two bangs

  No?

One bang

  Yes, it was not funny.

One bang

  Right. This is not easy, is it?

Two bangs

Was that "no, it's not easy"?

One bang

Yes, it was no.

One bang

This is a bit like Postman's Knock, isn't it?
Leo (*knocking three times*) Don't be so bloody stupid, woman.
Margot What's that, three bangs? Don't be so bloody stupid, woman?

One bang

(*With a sudden thought*) Oh Lord, you're not going to be stuck here for ever, are you? For all eternity.
Leo Not if I can bloody well help it.
Margot You could float off to the South of France.
Leo (*with one bang*) Together, why not? Just you and me.
Margot On the other hand, you might come in rather handy at the bridge table—I've had rather a losing streak lately... Hallo. Are you still there?

Leo is extremely frustrated, he pleads with Freda

Leo Please, Freda, tell her to stop blathering on. I want to talk about this kiss 'n' tell business. All those photos and letters and stuff.
Margot What's he saying?
Freda Er—he says he wants you to pay off my bar bill... £108.59p.
Leo You baggage.
Margot Oh, well, if that's what he wants.
Freda That's very sweet of you. (*A little joke*) A spirit who is generous with spirits.

They both groan

And he says he wants to talk about Sadie selling her story.
Margot You want to talk about the letters and things?

One bang

(*Finding them*) Here we are. You want me to try and stop Sadie talking to the press.

One bang

Isn't it a bit late to start worrying about your dirty linen?

Leo (*with three bangs*) Please, Margot, try to understand.

Margot Well, what the hell am I going to do?

Sadie enters overhearing this. She carries three drinks

Sadie What are you going to do about what?

Margot (*singing a line from* The Sound of Music. *Then*) What a dismal wretched morning, eh?

Leo gives one involuntary bang. Margot then Freda covers it with bangs of their own. A volley of taps. They raise their glasses and drink

Freda Is that for me? How lovely. You know when most people drink they start seeing things, but with me it's the other way round.

Margot So what have you decided to do? Have you done a deal with what's-his-name?

Sadie Graham Latimer. He's calling back in a minute.

Margot (*weighing the pile of letters*) He must have been quite in love with you.

Sadie I think so.

Leo This is damn confusing.

Margot I burnt all mine.

Sadie Why?

Margot I don't know, they're like old betting slips, aren't they, love letters. If you're on a winner you hand them in, and if you're not you throw them away. It's rather feeble, this trussing up of the past in elastic bands and shoe boxes, don't you think?

Leo She burnt my letters.

Sadie I suppose everything has its price. I've been offered fifty thousand pounds.

Margot gets her magnifier to one of the letters

Leo (*to Freda*) You were cheap at £108.59p.

Margot chuckles reading the letter. Sadie tries to retrieve it

Sadie No, please don't.

Margot For goodness sake, they're going to be read by twelve million people next Sunday. He had quite a nice turn of phrase, though, didn't he—I'm not sure there's a Z in "orgasm".

Freda What's that?

Margot No Z in "orgasm".

Freda Not in my day. Mind you, I haven't had one since the old king died.

Margot (*to Sadie*) Don't do it. Let me burn them for you. There's a brazier in the shed. Move on. Selling them would just look greedy and tacky.

Sadie And what about that snotty-nosed cow, his wife?

Margot What's that old saying, about the chap who goes looking for revenge...?

Leo He must dig two graves.

Freda (*without turning round*) He must dig two graves.

Margot That's it, he must dig two graves. That's what you'll be doing. One for yourself and one for the snotty-nosed cow. Don't do it, not if you want to make your mark as a serious actress.

Sadie I see what you mean. But from a business point of view, I'm still skint, aren't I?

Leo What's the form about back-dated cheques around here?

Freda (*whispering aside*) You're supposed to be in purgatory, not a casino.

Margot is inspired. She holds up the painting

Margot Yes... Well, look at this.

Sadie My God. The Augustus John. You were the mystery buyer.

Margot (*tapping her nose*) Yes, it was all a bit hush-hush. (*She hands her the painting*) I'd like you to have it.

Leo Her?

Sadie Me?

Freda Her?

Sadie I'm speechless.

Leo Me too.

Leo bangs his ashtray three times on Freda's table and Freda has to pretend she was killing a fly

Freda Margot, it's worth sixty-five thousand—have you gone stark raving mad?

Margot Very possibly.

Leo This is no time for her to start playing pass-the-parcel.

Margot Well?

Sadie You mean as a pay-off.

Margot Yes and no. I'd like you to have it. Sell it or hang it, I don't care. I've enjoyed meeting you ... you remind me of...

Sadie Of yourself?

Margot Just a bit. Back in the dark ages.

Leo I hadn't thought of that.

Sadie I don't know what to say. Don't you want it?

Margot I thought I did, but I don't. (*She peers at her own image*) What have
   you got to look so cocky about, my girl? Hmm? What do you know
   about—anything? You have it. I'm blind as a bat anyway. Sell it if you
   want.

Sadie gives her the wad of letters and stuff

Sadie Is this really a fair exchange?
Margot It might help towards the cottage. I'm sure it's what Leo would have
   wanted. Don't you agree, Freda?
Freda ⎫ (*together*) Absolutely. Absolutely.
Leo ⎭
Leo I'm overcome.
Freda I imagine he'd be overcome.

The phone rings. They all look at it. Margot answers it

Margot (*into the phone*) Hallo.

Sadie starts re-wrapping the painting

   This is Margot Buchanan's answering machine. I'm either... Oh, it's
   you... Hi there, scumbag. How are things? (*She looks round for Leo*) Yes,
   very sad. Very very sad...

Leo heads for the window with a zimmer frame in his hands

Leo I'm going to sort him out once and for all.

   Leo exits

Freda Leo. Leo... Come back. Come back.
Sadie (*comforting her; upwards*) Leave him, Freda. He's at peace.
Freda I don't think so.
Margot (*into the phone*) Yes... Quite a scoop for you, though, actually
   being here. ... Sadie? She's right here. Hold on.

Sadie hesitantly takes the phone. The painting is under wraps again

   After a moment, Judy enters

Sadie Hallo? Yes, it is. ... Very tragic, yes. (*She sees Judy*) Well, the truth
   is I hardly knew Sir Leo—I had a bit of a crush on him, of course. But
   nothing ever happened. He was married, for goodness sake. ... Yes, very

happily. ... Well, she's not at all snotty-nosed really. I actually came down to see Margot Buchanan. ... That's right—about *Romeo and Juliet*. No, not the cigars, the play. I'm an actress... (*She is clearly hearing an altercation on the phone*) What? ... Hallo. What's happening? ... What? (*To the others*) He says he's being attacked... What? ... By an invisible man with a zimmer frame...

Freda Oh my God...

Sadie (*into the phone*) What? ... He's taken your what?

We hear frantic screams off stage from a demented Graham Latimer. Sadie puts the phone down

Leo enters from the window, looking pleased with himself, something concealed behind his back

Leo (*as a headline*) "Scumbag Reporter Spooked by Old Luvvie with a zimmer frame..." (*He tosses a red toupee on to the floor*)

Everyone is gobsmacked, exclaiming "Wow", "Good heavens", etc.

(*To Freda*) Explain that away, clever clogs.

Freda It's a very tired gerbil that has been blown in by a freak gust of wind.

Sadie (*picking up the toupee*) It's a red toupee.

Margot picks up Sadie's mobile

Margot (*into the phone*) So now you know what it's really like to be exposed, spam-head. (*She hangs up*)

Sadie I better go and order my taxi. (*To Judy*) Goodbye, Lady Buchanan.

Judy Please come to the funeral, if you want to... Good luck with ... the cigars.

Sadie Thank you. (*To Margot*) Perhaps you'd better come and check out a matinée of *Romeo and Juliet* sometime.

Margot Yes, I'd like that.

Sadie No scowling.

They kiss

Margot Eyebrows up.

Sadie (*to Freda*) Take care, Freda.

Leo Can I say something?

Freda No.

Sadie (*kissing Freda*) No? OK. Suit yourself. Live dangerously.

Margot And be careful what you get up to in the interval on the first night.

Sadie (*giggling*) With my Romeo—absolutely.

Leo kisses Sadie's hand

> *Sadie reacts mildly as if to a fly landing on her hand, then exits not too unhappily*

Margot holds the letters. Freda goes to The Full Monty *jigsaw*

Judy (*to Margot*) I suspect you had something to do with that.

Margot (*patting the letters*) She's a nice girl.

Judy I'm very grateful anyway. I couldn't have coped with the humiliation as well as all the sadness... Of course, I knew there was someone else...

Leo Please, please, you must let me explain...

Freda No, no, no...

Margot What, darling? What's the matter, Freda?

Freda (*caught*) I am a daft old prune. I thought it was his head and it turns out to be his botty.

Leo Can I give you a hand?

Freda It's not a hand I'm looking for.

Judy I mean, all his friends thought he'd leave me years ago, his agent had a bet our marriage wouldn't last three years.

Leo I won a case of Dom Perignon.

Judy I've just always been so frightened of ... of making a fool of myself. I've never been very good at ... letting go. I kind of panic... (*This is hard for her*) Even my father used to call me Little Miss Prickly. I suppose I'm not really very lovable, am I?

Margot (*sweetly*) Well, not in an obvious sort of way—no. But *he* loved you, Leo, he really did... In fact that's why he came to see me.

Leo I beg your pardon?

Judy What do you mean?

Margot He wanted my help... He said—he'd been incredibly stupid and got himself into all kinds of trouble with a young girl. I didn't know then of course that it was Sadie, and he wanted to know how to put things right with you.

Judy That's why he came to see you? You can't be serious?

Leo You took the words out of my mouth.

Margot It would be too mean of me not to tell you, in the circumstances. He said the thought of losing you was unbearable.

Judy (*a lump in her throat*) I don't believe it. Leo said that to *you*?

Leo goes over to Freda and nudges her

Leo She's turned into Mother Teresa.

Margot (*remembering*) He said that at the end of the day you were two of a kind and he felt like just saying to hell with all the Hollywood crap, the salads and the hype and the whole bogus shebang of it. All he wanted was to be on a terrace in the South of France... (*She dries*)

Leo (*to Freda, lyrically*) With the sun setting on the sea in front of him...

Freda (*prompting her lyrically too*) With the sun setting on the sea in front of him.

Margot Exactly ... and a great wall of bougainvillea behind him—a glass of Pouilly Fuissé in his hand and you beside him playing backgammon in a daft old hat.

Judy I can just hear him saying it, you know.

Leo Pretty good stuff, huh?

Freda mimes vomiting and retires to her jigsaw

Judy I'd love to believe it.

Margot Why don't you? He was never going to leave you.

Judy (*very moved*) Well, that's ... um... Thank you for that. But you were wrong, though, about why I came to see you, I really did want to make amends.

Margot For taking Leo from me? He was past his sell-by date when you got him anyway.

Leo What am I, a prawn cocktail?

Judy No, not for taking Leo. You threw my birthday card in the bin. (*She gives the card to her again*) Open it. Please.

Margot All right. (*With the magnifier*) Lovely. (*Inside she finds a cheque*) What's this?

Judy A cheque.

Margot For sixty-five thousand pounds. Are you mad?

Leo They all are—it's an epidemic.

Judy It's from the sale of the painting. The money is yours by rights.

Margot Well, this really does make an awful lot of "mends".

Judy Good ... it was nothing personal, but would *you* want a picture of *me* hanging in your living-room?

Margot Perhaps not in the living-room, no.

Judy It is of you after all.

Margot Not really. Not the me I am now. It's of some other me, a me who believed in happy endings.

Leo (*to himself*) A beautiful kind person.

Margot Are you sure about this?

Judy nods

I'm very touched, and very grateful.

The two of them embrace tentatively. Leo is amazed

Leo It's like watching the Berlin Wall come down.
Margot I can still go on hating you though, can I?
Judy As much and as often as you like.
Margot If you'll excuse me... There's something I have to...
Leo You are marvellous. Here...

*Margot picks up the pile of Sadie's stuff and Leo passes her a box of matches.
Margot is surprised and pleased*

Margot You know something?
Judy What?
Margot The next time it's on the menu I'm going to give the spaghetti
bolognese a whirl.

Margot exits

Judy goes to Freda

Judy The funny thing is Leo knows perfectly well I don't play backgammon.
Freda Margot probably got that bit wrong—she's mad as a toothbrush.
(*Calculating*) With all that money I wonder if I could get her to buy me a
new CD player.
Judy Have you ever been married, Freda?
Freda Only three times. I didn't really get the hang of it. Have you ever
noticed how widows are a much happier breed than divorcees? Much less
sour and crabby. Why do you think that is?
Judy I suppose we'd rather have them dead than with another woman.
Leo The old scorched earth policy. Typical.

They are sort of doing the jigsaw together

Judy There are just so many things I'd like to say to him. Things I never got
round to.
Leo Such as what?
Freda Such as what?
Judy I don't know. I think I *am* a very irritating woman.
Leo Only a bit.
Freda I'm sure you're not at all.
Judy Always fussing and tidying and wiping everything in Dettol... I've
always liked things clean, you see... Leo'd have liked me to be a bit more
bohemian. You know, leave the top off things and use packet soups ... and

not play badminton every Thursday… And I wish I'd been able to make
him laugh the way other people did—he was always going on about how
funny Margot was. And … if I didn't say it very often it doesn't mean I
didn't … you know … love him… Mr Woodpecker.

Freda Mr Woodpecker?

Leo Oh, bloody hell. (*To his trouser front*) Why the hell couldn't you work
under a pseudonym once in a while.

Judy It was a silly private thing between the two of us. A nickname.

Freda (*she punches Leo*) Isn't that sweet. A nickname… (*She points to the
jigsaw*) For one of those?

The two women laugh. Leo peers at the puzzle

Judy Something like that. (*Peering*) Smaller.

Leo I'm very flattered.

Freda So is there anything else you'd say to him?

Judy Leo? That I'll miss him, of course. His awful jokes and kindness, and
the ghastly hollandaise sauce he liked to make and the way he always
blamed the dog for his farting.

Leo It *was* the dog.

The fire alarm goes off

Judy What's that?

Freda It's the fire alarm.

Judy You mean they're testing it?

Freda No, I don't think so. (*She looks out the window*) There's smoke
coming from the shed.

Leo Oh my God…

Someone off stage shouts "Fire"

Mrs Kidd hurries on

Mrs Kidd (*to an offstage figure*) There's no need to panic, Mr Nesbit… The
fire brigade is on its way. (*She goes to the window*) There's a fire in the
shed. Smoke.

Judy Flames too. Look.

Leo (*very alarmed*) That's not where Margot went, is it?

Freda (*very alarmed*) She's in there. Margot in the shed.

Mrs Kidd What… You both stay here…

Mrs Kidd runs off through the window

Sadie enters, she is in her coat or whatever and ready to go

Sadie What's going on?
Judy I thought you'd left.
Sadie My cab hasn't arrived. Oh, good heavens…
Freda Margot's started a fire. She's in there.

The two helpers, Robin and Francis, enter to check the rooms etc.

There is a feeling of urgency. Elderly offstage voices shout "fire" and then fade away. The siren of the fire engine can be heard approaching

In amongst all this activity Margot enters rather serenely. She is all in white and a little bemused

Nobody, including Leo for the moment, notices her

Judy Come on, Freda, we'd better get…

Mrs Kidd enters

Mrs Kidd The door is jammed shut. And I'm afraid that wretched journalist is there too… I'll have to get the firemen to…

Mrs Kidd exits to the hall

Margot is bemused

Margot What the hell is going on?
Judy Can't they knock the door down or something?
Margot (*not realizing she can see Leo*) I had a bit of trouble with the paraffin. It got a bit out of control…

Freda stops in her tracks

Freda Oh, no. Not you as well. Sod this for a game of soldiers.
Leo (*seeing her*) My God… Margot.
Margot I thought I was going to choke to… (*She slowly realizes*) Oh… Oh… I get it. I'm dead, am I?
Leo I'm afraid so, my darling.
Margot You mean I'm a…?
Leo We don't use the G word.
Margot (*to everyone*) Hallo… Coooeee… Hallo. Hallo.

Leo It's no use. It's worse than trying to get a drink in a theatre bar. Er ...
did they go up all right, my letters?

Margot Of course they did. It's all your fault I'm dead.

Mrs Kidd enters again

Mrs Kidd They're going to knock the door down. Perhaps you'd all better
go along to the dining-room... Miss Deacon...

Freda (*going to the invisible Margot*) Oh my poor poor Margot. I can't
bear it.

Mrs Kidd (*leading Freda off*) Come along, Miss Deacon. We'd better...

Margot I'm all right. Freda darling—I'm fine.

Leo We both are... Aren't we?

Leo and Margot smile broadly. Freda watches, thunderstruck

Sadie Freda... Freda...

Judy What's the matter with her?

Mrs Kidd Miss Deacon, are you feeling all right?

Freda (*perfectly normally*) Yes, I'm fine.

Mrs Kidd Come along then...

All except Leo and Margot go to leave the room

Freda turns back and picks up the cheque and takes it to Margot

Freda You couldn't just sign the back, could you? You won't be needing it
now.

Margot (*signing it*) Why not?

Freda Thanks.

Freda blows them a kiss and exits

Leo (*approaching Margot*) Well, here we are then.

Margot What's that supposed to mean?

Leo That was very sweet of you, what you did for my wife and ... um...

Margot Sadie.

Leo Sadie. Why did you do it?

Margot I suppose, just in case, on the off chance that either of those poor
misguided women loved you one fifth as much as I did.

Leo (*taking her in his arms*) Did? What do you mean *did*?

Margot All right then—do. Did. Always have.

Leo (*about to kiss her*) And me you, my darling.

Margot You don't think we should at least wait until after we've been buried.

The Lights slowly fade

CURTAIN

The first Curtain call is Margot and Leo re-playing the call they did together in Act I—complete with grimace etc.

FURNITURE AND PROPERTY LIST

Further dressing may be added at the director's discretion

ACT I

On stage: 2 chairs
Communal table. *On it*: **Freda**'s jigsaw puzzle of *The Full Monty*,
    small money box, ashtray
Freda's table. *On it*: **Freda**'s things
Theatrical memorabilia on walls
Highback chair
Margot's substantial table. *On it*: small telescope or opera glasses,
    magnifier, pile of papers, cordless telephone/ansaphone, wine
    gums, make-up, notepad, pen, betting slip
Vases with daffodils
Daily Mail newspaper
Box of Kleenex
Box of matches
Zimmer frame

Off stage: Bill (**Mrs Kidd**)
Pile of birthday cards (**Margot**)
Birthday card with cheque (**Judy**)
3 glasses of brandy on tray (**Mrs Kidd**)
Mobile phone, big bag and wrapped-up painting (**Leo**)
Mobile phone, shoulder bag containing bundles of letters, concertina
    strip of photographs, etc. (**Sadie**)

Personal: **Freda:** headset and hat (both worn throughout)
Mrs Kidd: pager
Margot: coins
Leo: false beard, tinted glasses, flask
Superman: paperwork

ACT II

Set: Inert substitute of **Leo**'s body on stretcher. *In its pockets*: wad of
money, packet of condoms, flask, half a bar of chocolate

Off stage: Cup of tea (**Mrs Kidd**)
3 drinks (**Sadie**)
Red toupee (**Leo**)

Personal: **Judy:** wrist-watch (worn throughout)

LIGHTING PLOT

Property fittings required: nil
1 interior. The same throughout

ACT I

To open: Spring sunshine

Cue 1   **All** are in a state of chaos   (Page 29)
             Fade lights down

ACT II

To open: Slowly bring up overall lighting

Cue 2   **Margot**: "…wait until after we've been buried."   (Page 61)
             Slowly fade lights down

EFFECTS PLOT

ACT I

ACT II